THE PASCHAL MYSTERY
IN PARISH LIFE

THE PASCHAL
MYSTERY
IN PARISH LIFE

HENRI OSTER

TRANSLATED BY

MICHAEL C. O'BRIEN

HERDER AND HERDER

1967

HERDER AND HERDER NEW YORK
232 Madison Avenue, New York 10016

Original edition: *Le Mystère Pascal
dans la Pastorale*, Paris, Les Editions du Cerf.
This edition has been revised by the author and
abridged with his permission.

Nihil obstat: Brendan W. Lawlor, Censor Librorum
Imprimatur: ✠ Robert F. Joyce, Bishop of Burlington
February 21, 1967

CONTENTS

THE PASCHAL MYSTERY
IN PARISH LIFE

INTRODUCTION

The paschal mystery is the very heart of Christianity. This is the formal testimony of Scripture.

In the minds of the apostles, Jesus definitively became the Saviour by his resurrection. On earth, he was the "servant" giving his life to redeem men, but glorified he is the Lord, the Saviour of each of the faithful through his divine power. God, by the very act of raising Christ from the dead and seating him at his right hand, gave men their Saviour, inaugurated the definitive era of the "Spirit" and "life."

To become more aware of this fact, we must take note of some of St. Paul's categorical declarations, such as: "If Christ has not been raised, your faith is futile and you are still in your sins" (1 Cor. 15, 17); "[Christ] died for all . . . and was raised" (2 Cor. 5, 15); "who was put to death for our trespasses and raised for our justification" (Rom. 4, 25); "if you confess with your lips that Jesus is Lord and believe in your heart that God raised him from the dead, you shall be saved" (Rom. 10, 9).[1] In fact, "in the theology of St. Paul the essential role attributed to the resurrection is our transformation into 'Christians.' This is the fount of life which makes us into new creatures."[2]

So we can say that, in substance, Christianity is the resurrection. It is a fact that the paschal mystery stands central in the economy of salvation. Since "the fulness of time" had come, the

1. See F. X. Durrwell, *The Resurrection*, New York and London, 1960, p. 26.
2. Lucien Cerfaux, *Christ in the Theology of St. Paul*, New York and London, 1958, p. 161.

9

realization of "the mystery of his will, according to his purpose which he set forth in Christ . . . to unite all things in him, things in heaven and things on earth" (see Eph. 1, 9 ff.), is a reality. Whether indeed "we consider individual destinies or the whole of the human race, all the rays of biblical tradition focus upon one unique mystery: the paschal mystery." [3]

Such, too, was the faith of the Church of the first centuries, and that Church is and will remain the Church's model for all time. This is the Church to whom the Church must always refer, to which she must ever have recourse if she is not to betray herself and her mission.

The most moving and, certainly, the most convincing witness of this faith is the art of the catacombs. This art, specifically funereal and clearly stamped with the seriousness of death, is essentially paschal. Not with angels in tears did the Church of the martyrs decorate the tombs. Nor, to console the parents of the dead, did she even present them with the statue of the *Pietà*. She presented the picture of the Good Shepherd gathering his sheep around him and giving them pasture in the fields of paradise; or again, the picture of mysterious "figures" of the Old Testament proclaiming the new life won by Christ, which his own with him have won too: Jonah cast upon the shore, Noah and his companions saved in the ark, Daniel in the lions' den.

In the age of Constantine, the Church had only to bring to fruition the heritage bequeathed her by the ages of persecution. It is magnificent how she was able to translate this essentially paschal faith into the mosaics with which she adorned the apses of her basilicas. As Jungmann has remarked of them, they give us "an impression of serene peace and solemn elevation" whose mystery is to be sought neither in the sparkle of the multicolored rocks nor in the harmony of the lines; their very content speaks. More precisely: these mosaics are not so much accounts of dra-

3. H.-M. Feret, "La mort dans la tradition biblique," in *Le mystère de la mort et sa célébration*, Paris, 1951, p. 133.

matic events, even those of salvation history, as they are simply representations of that which is. It is the epiphany of a "cosmos," of the Christian order of things that has been revealed to the Church, and she joyously and proudly proclaims it to whoever enters her sanctuary. The jubilation of color has become a profession of faith.

Always, whether symbolized by the cross or the lamb, or openly pictured as the Lord of Glory, Christ is the immutable center of the Church's mosaics. Always he is the redeemer, the mediator of salvation, the Lord of his people. Surrounding him are the redeemed: streaming from Bethlehem and from Jerusalem—from Judaism, from paganism—the sheep flock to him; harts descend the holy mountain and drink from the streams of paradise; everywhere the mystical vine extends its branches. And in ordered ranks on each side stand the apostles or certain other particularly venerated martyrs representing the people of the redeemed. In every instance, the accomplished redemption, the paschal theme, is what is placed before anyone in the basilica. Here, each day of the year, we celebrate the paschal mystery.

In this period, the same inspiration determined Christian art and the liturgical calendar. Until the fourth century, the paschal feast was *the feast* alone, and Sunday was considered the weekly Pasch.

The Church's prayer, too, was paschal. As a general rule, the posture for prayer was standing, turned towards the rising sun. The Council of Nice saw fit expressly to recall that on Sundays and during paschal time, standing should be the sole position for prayer (canon 20). Standing, like turning towards the east, was a generally widespread custom in antiquity, but soon it was given a remarkably fitting Christian interpretation. It was obvious: we are risen with Christ; that is why we stand. And if we turn towards the rising sun, it is because of Christ, the true sun who rose victoriously on the morning of the Pasch. Thus, too, "rising from on high" he will come again in the parousia to fulfill and manifest his paschal victory: "Risen with Christ and before seeking the things from on high, we stand as we pray not simply to remember this day is consecrated to the resurrection, to the favor bestowed upon us, but because the day itself seems a kind of image of the age to come." [4]

This same spirit was the soul of prayer itself. As we are about to see, the Roman liturgy in particular was able to maintain in unfailing continuity the paschal tradition of the primitive Church.

The early Church must have been well aware why she depicted the paschal Christ and his paschal work in the apses of her basilicas. She must have had some reasons for emphasizing the celebration of the Pasch which she prepared for forty days in advance and celebrated for fifty. Finally, she must have understood why she gave all her Sundays a fundamentally paschal character. This was the masterpiece of her educational system. This was how she taught her children their Christian dignity, and thus too did she impart to them that assurance, strong and serene, of Christian hope.

The Church's faith did not waver. Her prayer remained fundamentally the same. But for a number of reasons—which we shall later examine—it is evident that today many Christians do not at all think in the same way as their brothers of ancient times. Too often, Easter is considered but one feast among many others. It is agreed, of course, that Easter is "traditionally" the most important feast, but Christmas is much dearer to their heart. In some Christian countries, the solemnity of the Pasch can in no way measure up to the pomp of Corpus Christi. Such as these would at will put the feast of the Most Holy Trinity on equal rank with Easter because of its doctrinal depth, or that of the Sacred Heart for its religious richness.

There can be no doubt about it for anyone that this develop-

---

4. St. Basil, *Treatise on the Holy Spirit*, 27.

ment is deeply regrettable, for when one deserts the center for the periphery, he chances the loss of all. When the life-giving function of the heart is taken away, the body dies. Happily for Christianity and for us, however, the paschal mystery stands at the center of Christianity and can never be entirely taken away, even if pastors and faithful should one day lose sight of it completely.

Even so, it is now time for us to rediscover the scriptural and traditional concept of Christianity. The Church demands of us a strong gift of ourselves to this work. In fact, when Pius XII wrote his encyclical on the mystical body of the Lord, was not its meaning that we must take a new look at the supernatural structure in the Church whose head is the glorious Christ? When he restored the paschal vigil, and completely reformed Holy Week, was it not for the purpose of putting the paschal mystery back at the center of Christian faith and piety?

Thus, as Jungmann showed only a few weeks after the decree's appearance in November, 1955, its aim was eminently pastoral:

The most necessary thing for an understanding of the good news is an understanding in depth of the paschal mystery: not simply that Christ has risen and that one realize this fact with a feeling of pious contentment. He has risen for us, has passed through suffering's night and death itself to open for us the way to God. He lives and reigns forever—as we proclaim in the conclusion of the orations. He is the head of our Church, made "one" as his body; in grace we share his life and can ever enter into contact with him through the Church's sacraments.

Possibly many a pastor, turned grey under the harness in the Lord's vineyard, may object with a sigh: "But this is nothing new. I have been preaching this all the time; I have taught it to the children; I have proclaimed it a hundred times from the pulpit, but it is like talking to the wall, it will not penetrate either their heads or their hearts." Precisely here the decree of the Congregation of Rites comes to our aid. It starts from a certitude based upon secular experience: fundamentally, our faithful understand only what a feast celebrates. They understand the birth of Christ because there is the feast of Christmas; to some

13

degree they understand the Blessed Sacrament because of Corpus Christi. But we have as well a feast to celebrate the heart of Christian teaching, a feast lasting three days, and more than three days. However, this feast has been pushed to the side—and here the reform intervenes: its aim is to restore the feast to its rightful place so it can regain its radiant primitive force, so the faithful can, in celebrating it, rediscover the authentic message of Easter and, thus, the true joy and the true mentality of the Pasch—which is, more than anything else, the Christian mentality.[5]

That which already clearly appeared in the directives of Pius XII came to be solemnly proclaimed by the Second Vatican Council. With unparalleled clarity and vigor, the *Constitution on the Sacred Liturgy* affirmed the absolute predominance of the paschal mystery in Christian worship and in Christian life; for by it the work of redemption and the glorification of God were accomplished (see Art. 5). It is not surprising, therefore, that one finds the paschal mystery as a kind of directing principle throughout the constitution: in Article 6, concerning preaching and the liturgical celebration; in Article 10, apropos the eucharistic source of grace; in Article 61, regarding the paschal character of sacramental graces; in Article 81, where it is declared that the rite for the burial of the dead "should express more clearly the paschal character of Christian death"; and in the entire Chapter V, on the liturgical year.

In its *Instruction on the Sacred Liturgy,* on the implementation of the liturgical reforms outlined in the *Constitution on the Sacred Liturgy,* the Sacred Congregation of Rites declared:

5. . . . it is necessary first that all be persuaded of the intention of the *Constitution on the Sacred Liturgy* of the Second Vatican Council: not only to change liturgical forms and texts, but rather to stir up that formation of the faithful and pastoral activity which has the sacred liturgy as summit and fount (see *Const.,* Art. 10). The changes thus far introduced and to be introduced into the sacred liturgy in the future are directed towards this end.

5. "Die Reform der Karwochen-und Osterliturgie in pastoraler Sicht," in *Der Seelsorger,* February, 1956, pp. 197 ff.

6. The power of pastoral-liturgical activity rests in this, that the Christian life may express the paschal mystery in which the Son of God, incarnate and made obedient even to the death of the cross, is so exalted in his resurrection and ascension that he may share his divine life with the world. By this life, men, dead to sin and conformed to Christ, "may live no longer for themselves, but for him who died for them and rose again" (2 Cor. 5, 15).

This is done through faith and through the sacraments of faith, that is, chiefly through baptism (see *Const.*, Art. 6) and the most sacred mystery of the Eucharist (see *Const.*, Art. 47). Around the Eucharist are ranged the other sacraments and the sacramentals (see *Const.*, Art. 61) and the cycle of celebrations by which the paschal mystery of Christ is unfolded in the Church during the course of the year (see *Const.*, Arts. 102–107).

7. Therefore, even if the liturgy does not exhaust the entire action of the Church (see *Const.*, Art. 9), nevertheless, the greatest attention must be paid to the necessary connection between pastoral works and the sacred liturgy, so that pastoral-liturgical action is not exercised as if separate and abstract, but as intimately joined to other pastoral activities.

It is especially necessary that there be a close union between liturgy and catechesis, religious formation, and preaching.

8. Thus, the bishops and their assistants in the priesthood should relate their entire pastoral ministry ever more closely to the liturgy. In this way the faithful may derive the divine life in abundance from the perfect participation in the sacred celebrations, and, made the ferment of Christ and the salt of the earth, will proclaim the divine life and communicate it to others.[6]

In its own way, though unwillingly, the secular world also invites us to a "conversion," for it calls all religion into question. This threat irresistibly demands that we concentrate upon the essentials, and bring to light, in all their original boldness, the structural lines of the Christian cosmos; that we rediscover that concept of the Christian world that is both integral and complete. This does not mean burning what the Church has honored in the past, or destroying anything in the area of the faith where truth

6. The instruction can be found in *The New Liturgy. A Documentation, 1903–1965,* edited by R. Kevin Seasoltz, New York, 1966, pp. 515–534. See pp. 516–517.

can never become error, or ripping apart the realm of piety. But we have everything to gain in awakening more fully to a respect for the Christian order of things. The apostles preached the Risen One. Around him the primitive communities assembled. The risen Christ, the paschal Christ, remains forever the center of the Christian cosmos.

However, this is not at all a question of abandoning the historical Christ. Inasmuch as we live on earth, we must place our feet in his footsteps. Each one of his words is our light and life. We shall ever have need of the example he gave us in poverty and in labor, in dealing with men, and especially in his passion and death. The affirmation that his cross signifies the redemption of the world will always be the beginning and the end of every Christian proclamation. Yet for all that, it is not necessary to see the cross only under that aspect of mockery as it appeared to the high priests and the doctors of the Law. And if our faith never ceases to venerate the holy wounds of Our Lord and the pangs of his agony, there is nothing to stop us from seeing at the same time that these wounds radiate the glory of victory, and that his agony was "absorbed" in the jubilation of the "It is consummated." Roman art placed a crown upon the head of the crucified Lord and dressed him in a royal cloak; it again recognized the early primitive Christian adaptation of *Psalm* 95, 10: in truth, the cross is a throne; the liturgy has said it well: *"Regnavit a ligno Deus."* [7]

"He who finds his life will lose it, and he who loses his life for my sake will find it" (Mt. 10, 39). But it is only by seeing the Redeemer who has conquered death and who has paved the way to light, grace, and love that we can come to know that we do not follow this way in vain, and, at the same time, that we will find the strength to "commit" our lives to the service of his work and his kingdom.

7. Hymn "Vexilla Regis."

I.

THE PASTORAL MINISTRY
TODAY

The pastoral ministry includes the charge to teach the Christian people to live the "mystery." This means giving them a spirituality, and teaching them how to translate into their daily existence the new life given them by the faith and by the sacraments.

When we say that Christianity is in great need of rediscovering its paschal dimension, we logically affirm that, in the concrete, this "reconversion" is largely a pastoral concern. By so doing, we admit that the ministry has in some ways failed in its mission.

If we are willing to look at things squarely, there can be, in fact, no doubt that in the present pastoral ministry as a whole, the paschal mystery does not occupy its rightful place. This deficiency has been rectified indirectly, but in a particularly pointed way, by the reform of Holy Week and of the paschal vigil. In the mind of the Church, the precise aim of this reform is restoration of a more authentic, thus a more paschal, Christianity. Yet it is still the case in many parishes that, ten years after the reform, the paschal celebrations are reaching only a minority of the faithful, and that—even if they have been carried out correctly according to the rubrics (and this is not always the case)—they have not been able to give the participants the holy enthusiasm with which they overflow. We even dare to say that, in general, the paschal reforms of 1951 and 1955 have not as yet produced the result the Church anticipated. Most of the faithful were not prepared for these reforms because the pastoral ministry had not sufficiently familiarized them with the paschal mystery.

Let us not forget the fact that, objectively, the paschal mystery never completely lost its importance in the pastoral ministry—whatever the attempts even of right-intentioned persons to supplant it. No matter the effect of these attempts, Sunday, the Eucharist, and the sacraments must be celebrated, and the "ceremonies" of Holy Week and the paschal vigil have to be "carried out." There is more, and here we underline the paradox: even where no thought is given to the paschal mystery, where everything is done but what should be done, if the faith remains alive and if men are sanctified, if militant vocations are enkindled, this is yet due to the paschal mystery, and, in the last analysis, to it alone.

When we say that the paschal mystery does not have its rightful place, therefore, we mean this: that in the pastoral ministry, as it is understood and practiced by a great many priests, the paschal mystery is not clearly and unmistakably seen as the center which inspires everything, towards which all converges and from which all originates and takes its meaning. In this situation, the paschal mystery is but one "thing" among many and varied "things." By this very fact, it does not have that primary, central importance it really deserves in the mind of pastors, and, consequently, does not enjoy the role it ought to have in all their pastoral action.

The paschal mystery is indeed too austere to "please the people." Too, there is the practice of keeping the paschal celebrations and their preparation to the strict minimum, to what cannot be skipped. In justification it is said, in good faith, that the faithful have no taste for it, that they are too tired to stay up so late, and that, after all, it takes up a lot of time.

However, were our eyes more fixed on the unfolding of salvation history, we would undoubtedly recall more often one of its fundamental "laws," that of "apparent failure." Thus, both in our personal and in our pastoral life, the truer and more successful of our enterprises are those authenticated by God with this "trademark." Inversely, were we to live more in the spirit of salvation history, we would be led not to self-satisfied laziness, but to confidence. Heir of Israel and, like Israel, "chosen from among the nations" (as the name *"ekklesia"* says), the Church is entrusted with the work of being the priestly word-bearer of her people, delegated in their name for the true worship—thus bringing them salvation through the priesthood, even when she cannot visibly assemble them in her midst. Without doubt, this plunges us into the depths of mystery; but is not God greater than man, and, since Abraham, is not faith demanded of us? [1]

Harried by the urgency of our work, tormented by the immense spiritual and material misery inundating that humanity for whom we are responsible, we are not always sufficiently aware that besides the mystery of salvation there is a "mystery of lawlessness" (2 Thess. 2, 7). Although redeemed in principle, the world remains partly under the power of Satan and the cosmic "powers" (1 Cor. 2, 8; 10, 20; 12, 2; Eph. 6, 11–12); [2] in this world there are certain "values" that cannot be baptized. Then, too, we do not make ourselves sufficiently aware of the fact that, always, necessarily, frustrations are in store; the preaching of

1. In this regard, Karl Rahner has observed: "Just where is it written that *we* must have the whole hundred percent? God must have all. We hope that he takes pity on all and will have all indeed. But we cannot say that he is doing so only if we, meaning the Church, have everybody. Why should we not today alter to our use, quite humbly and dispassionately, a saying of St. Augustine's: Many whom God has, the Church does not have; and many whom the Church has, God does not have? Why, in our defeatism, which springs from a muddled feeling of pity for mankind, do we forget that it is not the truth but a heresy that there is no grace outside the Church?" In *The Christian Commitment,* New York, 1963, p. 35.
2. See Cerfaux, *Christ in the Theology of St. Paul,* pp. 301–302.

John the Baptist and of our Lord himself—and so every man announcing the Good News—began and must ever begin with the requirement of "conversion" (Mt. 3, 2; 4, 17). To enter the kingdom, man must be born again: "unless one is born of water and the Spirit, he cannot enter the kingdom of God" (Jn. 3, 5). And so it is with all these key texts in which the Lord constantly drove home the fundamental paradox of the Gospel; for example: "He who finds his life will lose it" (Mt. 10, 39); "unless a grain of wheat falls into the earth and dies, it remains alone; but if it dies, it bears much fruit" (Jn. 12, 24); "He who loves his life loses it, and he who hates his life in this world will keep it for eternal life" (Jn. 12, 25). It is necessary to be "converted," to deny one's self as the source of his own salvation and to open himself to the Saviour. It is necessary to accept being saved and perfected by grace. Capable of assimilating the whole world through culture; we must consent to being assimilated by God, and thus the supreme activity of man is that active passivity by which he consents to the work God does in him to draw him to his limits: "unless you eat the flesh of the Son of man and drink his blood, you have no life in you" (Jn. 6, 53).

In our concern to bring immediate aid to our brothers who are the victims of all kinds of injustices, and, at the same time, to make our Christian values incarnate in the world, we risk either forgetting or perverting Christian eschatology.

The Christian is not one who expects the coming of the golden age tomorrow. No longer is he one who lives in expectation of the heavenly city coming at the end of time. For him, the end of time has begun, the decisive event of history is the death and resurrection of Christ. That awaited is already given. The end of time is not a finish-line in the future, but the meaning of an action done today in reference to the Absolute. The Christian hope is the "hope of Glory" (Col. 1, 27).[3]

3. Note Doctrinale (of the French hierarchy), *Construction du monde et croissance du Royaume*, p. 526.

We could continue analyzing in this way the temptations always awaiting us and how we fall into them, but that is enough. One last admission, however, must be made. In the thousand-faceted ministry we have been talking about, there is a wrong, almost an injustice: an essential, fundamental, practically forgotten fact which takes a back seat. It is the "mystery," better the perfection of the "mystery," for us, in us, this very day, at this precise moment of salvation history wherein we are placed—a perfection actualized in the *hodie* of the liturgy through the word and the sacrament. This question is of such importance that we shall return to it later.

When we see the ministry as it thus appears today, we are not at all surprised to see the small role the paschal mystery plays in it. Yet the absence of this mystery, which is, as Louis Bouyer has said, "nothing else than the Christian mystery seen in its heart and unity," [4] truly has a tragic character. It is to the study of the causes of this absence that we will now devote our attention.

The reasons why our pastoral ministry is deficient are numerous and of many kinds. We pretend certainly neither to enumerate them all nor line them up according to their true importance. One thing, however, is clear: with possibly one or two exceptions, those we mention are all of the theological order. This is not surprising, for whenever doctrine is at fault or contains, if not errors, at least imperfections or lacunae, then the pastoral ministry, spirituality, and concrete Christian life inevitably are full of parallel shortcomings.

1. DOGMATIC THEOLOGY

We must begin our examination with dogmatic theology, the foundation and source of all other theological disciplines. And

4. *Introduction to Spirituality,* New York and London, 1961, p. 113.

21

we will take our lead from a work of Karl Rahner, his contribution to the collection *Paschatis Sollemnia.* In it, as he says, he has posed a certain number of "dogmatic questions apropos of paschal spirituality."[1]

Rahner begins this essay with an affirmation quite eloquent in itself: even in the most recent dogmatic manuals, he writes, the resurrection occupies a ridiculously insignificant place. Although all treat lengthily of Good Friday, they dispose of Easter in a few lines—if they mention it at all. Is it to be wondered at, then, that the paschal mystery occupies such a peripheral place in the thought of so many pastors when their dogma courses relegated it to insignificance? Nevertheless, it is the "fulcrum of salvation history" and dogmatic theology should have much to say about it. In fact, it does not; why not is the heart of Rahner's investigation.

According to him, there is, first of all, a "very curious division of labor" resulting from a perfectly valid evolution in the teaching of theology. As it happened, apologetics and fundamental theology were separated from dogmatic theology around the end of the eighteenth century and became autonomous disciplines. Since it had to establish a solid foundation for Christianity, fundamental theology appropriated the resurrection to itself as the outstanding proof of the mission of the divine legate. Though indeed legitimate in itself, this appropriation brought consequences as damaging as they were unexpected. Knowing that the resurrection was treated in the apologetics course, the professor of dogma could think himself dispensed from talking about it in his turn. In so doing, he forgot that apologetics, by its very nature, could not do justice to the real content of the resurrection, for apologetics' role is to see it solely under the formal, powerfully "leveling" aspect of a miracle. It was easy, then, to reach the

1. "Dogmatische Fragen zur Osterfrömmigkeit," in *Paschatis Sollemnia,* edited by Balthasar Fischer and Johannes Wagner, Freiburg, 1959, pp. 1–12.

point of believing it enough to grant the resurrection's historic reality, and, perhaps, to show how Christ, through it, won his bodily glorification by title of personal merit. With this outlook, dogmatic theology said nothing more than fundamental theology. Finally, in the tract on general eschatology, dogmatic theology treats of the resurrection and glorification of humanity, but since it has already spoken about the Risen Lord, why should there be this repetition? Yet, just for example, the progress of biblical theology has shown us that we have no right to reduce the resurrection to so meager a place.[2]

As real as they were, these superficial and exterior causes could not have been the determinants. There are others, more essential and more ancient. With the exception of St. Thomas and, in the post-Tridentine period, Suarez, the interest and work of dogmatic theology were practically centered on the Lord's incarnation and death. As a result, Rahner says, Christology came to neglect the other mysteries of Christ's life: his circumcision, baptism, transfiguration, and so forth. These it abandoned to exegetes and the meditations of pious souls. It is not surprising that the resurrection fared no better. And this admission invites another question: Whence came this lack of interest in dogmatic theology for those mysteries other than the incarnation and death?

Rahner sees a fundamentally Western attitude at the root of this peculiar phenomenon. This attitude clearly sees Christ as the teacher and founder of the Church, but it seeks understanding and explanation of the redemption and the properly soteriological role of the Lord "in the framework of a purely juridical theory of satisfaction." In reparation for the sin of humanity, God required satisfaction and brought it about in Christ's death on the cross. If God grants our salvation in this way, and in this way alone, all the other mysteries appear simply as preparations

2. See Durrwell, *The Resurrection*, for example (note by Fr. Rahner).

for the essentially salvific action found in the cross alone. Good Friday, therefore, and it alone, is decisive.

In conformity with ancient liturgical tradition, we indeed continue to proclaim the Pasch as the Christian feast par excellence. But really, Good Friday is the true "feast." In our piety, the crucified, the "man of sorrows," nourishes our meditation almost exclusively; he receives all our love.

A decade before Karl Rahner's work, I.-H. Dalmais already remarked that

the predominant role given in the Latin Middle Ages to the redemptive passion and to its meritorious and satisfactory character, did not, perhaps, retain respect for the total outline of the divine plan of salvation which makes possible an understanding of its liturgical expression.[3]

So, too, as it contributed to reducing the theology of the resurrection almost to non-existence, the satisfaction-theory prevented elaboration of a truly satisfactory theory of the liturgy. It forced those seeking to account for the liturgical mystery to have recourse to what Dalmais calls desperate expedients.

It is perfectly logical that the satisfaction theory lead to these impasses. Rahner explains it thus:

This purely juridical theory of satisfaction is based upon the following tacitly admitted principle: that God could have chosen any satisfactory act of the God-man as the act of redemption, provided it be made worthy of God by the dignity of the person carrying it out. But, concretely, God decreed that it be the death on the cross. All the rest flows logically from this. In reality, Easter is now of interest only for Jesus' private personal destiny and can no longer have importance for salvation. We are all the more able to find here a *confirmatur* for the detailed explanation given to Good Friday. If the Reformation Churches have made Good Friday their principal feast, and if, in his efforts at "demythologization," Rudolf Bultmann seems to focus his theology and faith exclusively upon the cross and away from Easter, these are but the extreme consequences of that redemption-theology, purely juridical in

3. "Le 'mystère,' Introduction à la théologie de la liturgie," in *La Maison-Dieu*, 14 (1948), p. 74.

nature and based upon a somewhat arbitrary decree of God. We could trace the line of this tendency back through St. Anselm and St. Augustine, to the origins of a peculiarly occidental theology in Tertullian and St. Cyprian. And this is a theology in which (even if, to be sure, it does not realize it, through the hardening of a reflex principle bordering on heresy) the incarnation has no purpose beyond providing the subject. If this subject so wishes and if God consents to accept his work as that of all humanity, he can accomplish equivalent satisfaction as reparation for the offense given to God. According to all the evidence, Western theology remains in the logic of the system, declaring that the incarnation of the Word was willed by God solely with a view to the destruction of sin. On this basis, we can easily see that Western theology is a bit embarrassed when confronted with the problem of understanding the present role of the risen and glorified Lord. In fact, the blessedness he enjoys in heaven in his glorified humanity seems to be a personal happiness uniquely for himself. There is indeed the Thomistic thesis that Christ's humanity has a permanent and "physical" role of mediation after his resurrection and glorification. Too imprecise in itself and constantly discussed, however, this doctrine has been unable to inform Christian existence and piety.

In addition, to characterize the blessedness of the redeemed in heaven, theological speculation has taken the notion of an immediate vision of God as its starting point (*mulla mediante creatura in ratione objecti visi se habente*[4]). In this, once more, we see no place for our Lord's humanity. With this kind of perspective, it is hard to recognize any permanent salvific role for the glorified Lord. At the same time, his continual intercession so clearly affirmed by the Scriptures (see Jn. 14, 2 ff.; 14, 16; 16, 7; Rom. 8, 34; Heb. 7, 25; 9, 24; 1 Jn. 2, 1), as well as the happiness resulting from communion with his humanity, tends to become the allure of simple anthropomorphisms. Under these conditions, Western piety, neither able nor desirous of departure from Christ, and finding insufficient nourishment in the contemplation of his earthly life alone, not surprisingly became focused upon the real presence of Jesus in the Eucharist. There at least we feel close to him. According to J. A. Jungmann, this forgetfulness of Christ's salvific role—in its turn cause for the obscurity of the true meaning of Easter—originated in the Western defense against Arianism.[5] By this they came to see in Christ

4. Denzinger, no. 530.
5. *Pastoral Liturgy,* New York and London, 1962, pp. 1 ff.

only "God with us," with the consequence that his role as mediator necessarily had to pass more or less into the background.

All this is in accord with what we said above, at least in that, for the Western theology of the redemption, the decisive point is precisely the dignity of the divinity of the person; and because this is so, the particular intra-Trinitarian relation between the Father and the Son plays no indispensable and necessary role.[6] This corresponds perfectly with the basic attitude of Western theology in the sense that since St. Augustine (taking him as the counterpoint to previous theology), it is considered to go without saying that each divine person could have appeared hypostatically in the world. Thus, properly speaking, the mission of the Son in the world does not prolong the "position" of intra-Trinitary mediator of the Logos.

On this basis, one could, moreover, ask whether these factors which have contributed since the time of St. Augustine in reducing the mediatory role of Christ should be laid at the feet of Augustinian anti-Arianism. But although, in all these questions, anti-Arianism played an effective role, and although it consequently contributed to the atrophy of paschal theology and spirituality, it is far from being seen as the adequate explanation of the historic phenomenon in question. In fact, H.-J. Schulz, a disciple of Jungmann, has in a remarkable work [7] raised the question: How can it be that in the East, as the very liturgy bears witness, an emphatically cosmic spirituality can be on a par, without any difficulty, with an evidently equally pronounced spirituality of the divinity of Christ—all this in the same liturgy which, by that fact, relegates the true mediatory function of Christ between God and man to the background? With the question expressed in this way, Schulz thought he found an answer in neo-Chalcedonianism. In other words, the Alexandrine-Cyrillian theology, while maintaining Chalcedonian orthodoxy (with its insistence upon the two natures unmixed in Christ), put the accent upon the divinization of the created by the divinity who assumed it, and this more clearly than unmitigated Chalcedonian theology had done. It could better comprehend, on this basis, how

6. Rahner writes in a footnote: "Striving at all cost to maintain its thesis that the redemptive sacrifice was equally offered to the Logos himself, Western theology has been constrained to speak of a double moral 'subject' in Christ, a conception which permits, nonetheless, each of the other persons of the Trinity (or the one God who will be simply monotheist and who will become man) to receive a like satisfaction."

7. Rahner cites Schulz's "Die 'Höllenfahrt' als 'Anastasis,'" in ZkTh, 81 (1959), pp. 1–66.

the cosmic process of the divinization of the created, begun by the incarnation and bridging the abyss separating God and the creature, was definitively effected in the resurrection.

Schulz's theory is enticing. We might say it answers a question one would never clearly formulate for himself if he did not know in advance, as a possible answer, the solution offered by neo-Chalcedonianism. All the same, we must ask if this answer is really exact and especially if it is adequate. For one could, with a hint of skepticism, ask whether such a subtle nuance in Christology (of which we have become fully aware only recently) could have anything to do with explaining such important and manifest differences between the paschal spiritualities of the West and the East.

One could then ask, precisely because of its accentuated anti-Arianism, if the West did not in fact also know something of a neo-Chalcedonianism in Christology. How does it then happen that we do not see here the same consequences which Schulz believes necessary to attribute to it in the East? Again one might ask whether we should not see in neo-Chalcedonianism an effect rather than a cause of a fundamental religious and theological attitude which is present in the East but lacking in the West; which, in the East, manifests itself in the force of its paschal spirituality, but is *de facto* lacking in the West even if it is equally possible to uncover a notional and theoretical neo-Chalcedonianism in Western theology. Actually, it seems improbable that one could deny that the theology of the redemption, in both East and West, already exhibited these differences in an age prior to these differing developments in Christology—in other words, that from the fifth and sixth centuries the West thought rather in juridical and moral categories, while in the East, even though there the cross was still perfectly understood, the redemption had been considered as a really ontological process which, begun by the incarnation, is fulfilled in the divinization of the world (not just in the forgiveness of the fall), and which established itself victorious for the first time in the resurrection of Christ (not just in the expiation of sin on the cross).

Such, says Rahner, are the historical factors which reduced paschal theology and, consequently, paschal spirituality to near nothingness. In the course of his article, he also raises some "objective questions with regard to the very content of paschal dogma."

First, Rahner states that the theology of the Pasch presupposes a theology of death—which, practically speaking, remains to be developed. In fact, to understand the mystery of the resurrection, it is indispensable beforehand to understand the mystery of Good Friday and Holy Saturday. This presupposes that theology cannot be content to investigate the passion which precedes the death, but must attack the very essence of death. But up to now this it has not done. For all practical purposes, theology has seen nothing in Christ's death but the (to some extent fortunate) completion of his sufferings, and to these last alone is it limited when it speaks of Christ's death and his soteriological role.

Under these conditions, says Rahner,

. . . it is clear that this theology of Christ's death has an object which cannot be essentially delineated from any other work done (or possibly done) by Christ during his earthly life, and so its salvific role can be determined only by reference to criteria of the moral order. By doing so the true meaning of death is passed by, and chances are this same mode of action (reference to criteria of the moral order) will be justified by explaining that, in a theology of the soteriological role of Christ's death, an object with a moral role is necessary. This cannot be death in itself (since in itself it is only the passively undergone separation of the body and soul), but must be the sufferings which preceded it and which alone gave Christ the occasion to exercise his obedience and love.

In this process, there is the danger (not in words but in fact) of reducing the theology of Christ's death as such to nothing. This makes it necessary, first of all, to get as exact as possible an idea of death itself. This is the only starting point from which we can elaborate a true theology of the death of Christ.

This is far more possible today than in the past. Ladislaus Boros in his *The Mystery of Death* has shown that modern philosophy is resolving the problem of methodology which has been an obstacle up to the present. In fact, philosophical reflection—an indispensable prerequisite for theological reflection—

seemed at a loss because man has no direct experience of death. In observing someone die, we have no experience of death itself. We see only the exterior aspect, the biological and psychic "prelude" to death. This is no longer the case, however, since the works of Heidegger, Blondel, Joseph Maréchal, and Gabriel Marcel have removed the methodological obstacle just pointed out. Some theologians have profited from this, such as Robert Gleason, and especially Karl Rahner and Ladislaus Boros.[8]

In the article from which we continue to quote, Rahner applies the results of these researches on death itself to Christ's death:

It could well be that we cannot adequately define death as being only the "separation of the body and the soul." It is indeed the state in which man touches the depth of his most extreme powerlessness and in which he sees himself left defenseless before the nameless mystery of his existence. But if death, taken strictly for what it is and from a point of view based upon the reality itself, is equally the supreme human act, the act in which one disposes of his entire past life gathered in the ultimate decision of his liberty, and if man's eternity thus reaches maturity, then the human death of Christ, too, is certainly not just some kind of a moral act Christ performed before he really died. It is much rather, as such, the total act of Christ's life, the definitive act of his freedom, the complete integration of his temporality into his human eternity.

If this is true (we can no more than raise the problem here), then Christ's resurrection is not a new event tacked on *after* his sufferings and death, but indeed (in spite of that temporal extension which is a constitutive factor even of the most homogeneous and indissociable act of man carried out in space and time [9]), it is the epiphany of what was

8. See Ladislaus Boros, *The Mystery of Death,* New York and London, 1966; Robert W. Gleason, *The World to Come,* New York and London, 1958; Karl Rahner, *On the Theology of Death,* New York, 1961.

9. Rahner explains in a footnote: "In itself, it should be easy to make a Scholastic philosopher understand that, having already reflected on the essence of (spatial and temporal) continuity, a thing or an event, is not necessarily independent of or completely other than another thing or event merely because it comes after or this other which precedes it in time. These can be temporal factors in a strictly homogeneous event which, although extended

accomplished in Christ's very death: the active and passive reinstatement of this true man's total reality in the mystery of the merciful love of God, a reinstatement worked through Christ freely disposing of his life and total existence.

In this perspective, Good Friday and Easter are seen as two complementary aspects of one strictly unique event in the existence of Christ. No longer can we have the impression that basically Good Friday, by itself, could have a salvific role (as satisfaction offered to God's offended majesty) even if the Pasch had not followed. This deceptive appearance removed, the soteriological role of Easter (which by far and essentially surpasses its importance for apologetics and for the Lord's personal happiness) stands in clear relief. By the very fact that a portion of this world, possessed by the power of Christ's liberty (liberty unlimited and free from all concupiscence), has been totally reinstated, in its fullest reality (and this in the most perfect obedience and love), in the "disposition" of God—by that total disposition of which man is capable only in the act of death—the *Pasch* and the redemption of the world were accomplished. For, not just as the result of some juridical acceptance on the part of God, but in its very essence, the resurrection is the event by which God not only "assumes" irrevocably the creature in its own reality (this was already accomplished in the incarnation), but through which he divinizes the creature to the point that this glorification is realized in the acceptance by the free creature of this divine "acceptance."

This statement makes sense if we take note of the two following things: in a world characterized by man's fall, the free creature's parallel acceptance of the divine "assumption" is necessarily death, which, therefore, becomes the birth of the liberated life; in the second place, Jesus represents a real element of the physical world. He is a member of humanity viewed in its biological aspect; he is a son of Adam born of woman, a member of the human community, a community for salvation as well as for destruction. But the physical, spiritual, and moral unity of the world is such that the ultimate choice of the man Jesus is ontologi-

---

in time, cannot be separated in its essence. In order to be a unit, the factors of a being (at least of an event) need not coexist at an arbitrarily chosen moment. Allow us to recall that modern physics seems, even for time in physics, to know of ultimate temporate atoms which are really not divisible, although they 'endure' and are made up, apparently, of even smaller particles of time."

cally (and not just as the result of a juridical disposition on the part of God) the beginning—irreversible and already containing the end in itself—of the transformation and the divinization of *all* created reality. (In saying this, we do not deny, but on the contrary positively affirm the unity of the world in all its dimensions, affirm that the fact that Christ is really and ontologically a member of this one world results from a free disposition of God. But this disposition does not add something juridical and notional to the world; it puts the world in a framework essentially its own.)

To make this better understood, Rahner quickly brings up the idea of sacrifice. He points out that the only true sacrifice is that in which man's gift is really transferred from the profane sphere to the sacred, to God's "possession." That is, it must be truly transferred into the very interior of God's exclusive "disposition." Thus, God's acceptance of the gift is not a consequence which more or less surely results from man's act; it is of the very essence of sacrifice that it be accepted. Sacrifice and accepted sacrifice are not two different things. To make this possible, it is necessary that God himself establish the conditions permitting man to offer in such a way as to have God's acceptance, that God enable man to offer sacrifice by instituting the priesthood. When the required conditions are fulfilled, that is, when the liturgical symbolism is carried out "in spirit and truth" (Jn. 4, 23), God's acceptance cannot be reduced to a purely juridical fiction; on the contrary, this acceptance must be real. Since this acceptance is part of the very essence of the sacrifice, it follows that the gift offered (in the Christian dispensation especially, nothing other than man himself) enters totally, in all its ramifications and concrete reality, into the pure "disposition" of God who has chosen to accept it. And this leads to the conclusion Rahner has thus formulated:

Being "accepted" completely, without reserve—and definitively—by the God who, through his grace, reveals and communicates himself, is equivalent to man's being glorified in his total reality, and thus to being definitively raised up and "exalted" through death. So the sacrifice of

31

Good Friday is truly perfected in itself only when it is the sacrifice "accepted" in the event of the Pasch. These three days (Good Friday, Holy Saturday, and the Pasch), what is celebrated in a holy anamnesis, is this unique, identical, total, salutary event which remains strictly one, even when it "endures" in order to be itself.[10]

For Rahner, this analysis of the very essence of sacrifice provides a point of departure for a new theological reflexion running in two opposite directions. To his way of thinking, it was a practice in the early Church to go back in some way to the sources to rethink in a new, basic manner the very essence of the incarnation. He saw in this research a possibility of shedding new light on the "destiny" of Jesus, on the soteriological meaning of this destiny, and, in particular, on that of the resurrection. The second path of research concerned the glorified Saviour's permanent mediator function—accomplished but not yet perfected—in favor of man, and for all times.

He thinks it necessary to pose the following question with regard to the first of these problems:

How are we to understand the incarnation of the Word, how are we to understand the assumption of human reality and the essence of this reality itself in such a way that, from the very beginning, the event of the incarnation can be conceived as not only the assumption of a real thing of a static nature, but rather the assumption by the Word of a time, of a history, of a life-giving death? And then, how are we to understand that by the very essence of the incarnation (since it is in itself a formally soteriological event), this other event of the death and resurrection is willed and assumed? Wherever a man's history, the action of his liberty and the absolute summit of this action of liberty, are conceived as not an event resting on the foundation (itself not affected) of a human nature seen in a material and static perspective, but on the contrary as the act of a being who realizes himself in them and who finds his own proper reality only through them—if we see in liberty not so much a "power" that one *has,* but the "disposing" liberty which one

10. See on this subject, for example, M. de la Taille, *The Mystery of Faith,* vol. 1, theses xii–xv, pp. 183–255 (note by Fr. Rahner).

is [11] in view of bringing his own being as such to its full perfection, and which is given in advance—then the event of the incarnation is far more closely and essentially united to the perfection of the assumed human life than in the case where the incarnation is considered simply as the bringing into existence of a human subject in whose life, and only in what is to follow, such and such a thing will happen.

The other course of suggested research goes in the opposite direction:

Again, if we begin with an exact interpretation of Christ's death, and if we do not see in what comes "after" his death an event which, in the time which continues, can only be annexed to the event of the death, but on the contrary we see here the definitive state of his earthly life having come by death to its full maturity and to its real perfection, then it is necessary that the Lord—who remains—fulfill a real and equally permanent salvific role without which there would be no possibility of attributing such a role to his death. By the fact that death is the end of time (in that it definitively bounds it and thus opens eternity), what "follows" death (and the resurrection which is an essential element of *this* death) is exactly what is definitively accomplished in death. And, inversely: what is here accomplished is the definitive, and thus it is that which truly and forever "is" and acts. The life of the Lord in glory is not a personal and private recompense for something he has accomplished during his earthly life and which has only those "consequences" which, now that their cause belongs to the past, have continued to subsist for themselves. On the contrary, this life in glory is the very reality of the

11. Rahner writes in a footnote: "Evidently, this word must be understood with the reservations necessary for statements of this type when, in contradistinction to the absolute God, we are dealing with a finite creature. But this difference ought not to make us forget an *act* posited by an intrapersonal being implies a relation with this being essentially more external than is the case for the being by itself and it realizes itself more freely. In this case, the being is 'confided' to itself. Though liberty cannot effectively 'destroy' it, nor suppress it, it is no less true that this being is affected as such by the free act. He does not just 'carry out' this act, but, in a certain sense, he becomes it himself. Thus, a man does not just *have* bad acts, but by them he himself becomes bad. For this reason, the inverse is equally true: in that in which a spiritually free being is willed and accepted, his own realization is, by that very fact, not only 'made possible' and (eventually) foreseen, but willed and accepted."

soteriological role of his earthly life "accepted" by God in its liberated efficaciousness and in its efficacious reality.

Evidently, it is necessary to try to make more precise the idea of what this efficacious reality of a soteriological nature is. Here is the place to examine how we can make it comprehensible that Jesus' humanity continues to play a role precisely there and at the very moment that the infinite reality of the eternal God offers himself in an immediate manner for the vision and the happiness of the saints. In other words, it is necessary to show that in the incarnation and in its fulfillment by the resurrection, the glorified human reality of Jesus' body can be, in a real and permanent manner, the mediation of the "immediate" of God. It is then necessary to establish that the communication of supernatural grace to the creature, essentially founded on the hypostatic union and on nothing else,[12] is equivalent to an unmediated whose ontological prerequisite is given by the notion of a communicated unmediated. Every unmediated is, in effect, unmediated *with regard to* someone. The

12. Rahner writes in a footnote: "One is, however, right in supposing the relation existing between the incarnation and the gift to man of supernatural grace is not just a relation of event, but an essential relation. From the viewpoint of the hypostatic union, it is highly improbable that this statement will meet with objections from theologians. Everyone will admit (unless he would fall into an unexpressed Nestorianism, and unless he would contradict the last intentions of Cyrillian Christology) that Christ's human nature must be divinized equally in what is most interior to it by what we call sanctifying grace. But we must note that this human nature as a member of humanity (which can be demonstrated in a transcendental deduction from the fact, for man, of being "organized" in view of dialogue and of being a sharer, of having the character of being a dialogue-partner) is essentially a member of this humanity; and, by that fact, this human nature (as nature!), in its final destination cannot abdicate the context of the meaning this one and total humanity has. Thus we come to realize that the divinization of the Word's human nature necessarily signifies the vocation of all men to a supernatural community of communion with God. Beginning from this, it does not seem we are going too far in also supposing a necessity in the opposite direction. Where there is to be a supernatural participation in God's own life through a true communication of himself which God accords to men, there should be also incarnation (it being well understood that one and the other, inasmuch as they are one and are connected, remain clearly free, and that the necessity in question is the necessary consequence of something which, in itself, is free and not necessary). Yet, to see this more clearly, it is necessary to show that the hypostatic union is the necessary mediation towards that immediateness which is given in the immediate vision of God (which is itself the highest actuality of grace)."

requirement here of a certain mode of existence, a certain disposition, etc. in the one with whom there is to be an unmediated rapport does not at all contradict this unmediatedness, but is its necessary prerequisite. That is the reason why, for example, even in the full Council of Vienne, theological tradition admitted the *lumen gloriae* as a prerequisite to the immediate vision of God and had no notion of a contradiction opposing this notion to the immediate character of the vision, although the *lumen gloriae* was considered a created reality. It is the mediation of the "immediate" of God, pure openness: it is precisely this type of strictly supernatural "thing" which, by itself, as differentiated from the natural (and this by virtue of a properly formal causality of God in contradistinction to a simply efficient causality), does not lead back to God in the sense that he is its infinitely distant source, but he himself is the gift, absolutely, because it itself exists only through the absolute communication which God gives of himself. Working from these presuppositions, we are in a position to sound the relations existing in the *lumen gloriae,* the mediation of the unmediatedness of God on one side, and the glorified humanity of the Lord on the other, for which we have just revindicated a permanent mediator function in the communication of the unmediated of the vision of God—if we can truly and effectively speak of a permanent mediatory function of the God-Man, and if this function is not to be excluded from that which, all the same, constitutes the essence of salvation and supernatural beatitude, that is to say, of the immediate vision of God. It is only if the Lord, risen and exalted to the right hand of God, remains the permanent and always efficacious "access" to God (an access through which it is always possible to go once again, which can never be of the past, which can never remain behind us as a road we have already travelled, but must never cease to show us the Father), and only on that condition, that the paschal mystery is understood for what it is: the perfection of the world in God who is truly all in all through the event of Easter, an event already begun but which is still on the way to perfection in us.

Although there is always a relation between an event and its effects, between that which is produced and that which results from it, this relation is not always the same. In fact, as Rahner says, events have two aspects. Some bring about consequences which continue to exist in the very time in which they were produced; these effects which "last," by that very fact, ceaselessly take on a new and different destiny and are thus no longer what was effected in the event: thus the event itself falls completely into the past. On the other hand, the event is the source of a definitive eschatology. An event of this nature is "close to" its effects in a different way than an event of the former kind. What it engenders does not, properly speaking, "continue"; the result is definitive. By this very fact, an event of this type cannot fall back into a state of "having been."

Clearly, this would be the place to develop these reflections and make them precise. Such as they are, they nevertheless permit us to see how, in an ontologically unique and unequaled manner, the event of the Pasch remains "present." Since the paschal feast is celebrated in a true "anamnesis," [13] it has a direct and essential relation to the paschal event itself. That is precisely what gives this celebration its unique character: "The anamnesis and that which is made present through it in the celebration mutually condition each other," Rahner says. To his way of thinking, the perspective thus opened permits us to show as well in what manner the Eucharist is itself the celebration of the paschal mystery. It is in no way reduced to a mere reference to an apparently past event; on the contrary, it is the presence of that which was accomplished on Easter to be definitively that which constitutes the "validity" of the event itself.

Understood on these bases, the paschal feast will appear as the highest expression of that which is celebrated in a true anamnesis in each celebration of the Eucharist: the unique event of the death and resurrection which, in the physical world, had an evidently passing character (see Rom. 6, 9; Denz. 2297), but which, and rightly so, "had to" pass so the definitive could rise and remain, but which also essentially "remains"—*because of this,* this unique event can be "celebrated."

13. See Rahner's definition of this word in his *Theological Dictionary,* New York and London, 1966.

2. THEOLOGY OF THE LITURGY

We cannot say of this theology that it has gone astray on important points; we are simply forced to say that it does not exist. We are the more astounded at this monumental lacuna in the teaching of theology when we recall that the Fathers did indeed have an authentic theology of the liturgy. Perhaps it was not elaborate and in tract form, but it was everywhere present in their mystagogies and consequently in their way of living the liturgy with their people. We should be equally surprised to affirm that, except for those centuries of apathy, the liturgy itself preserved sufficiently clear vestiges of the patristic concept. To demonstrate this, we cite nothing more than one small phrase from the Secret of the Ninth Sunday after Pentecost, for it truly condenses a complete theology in a few words: "May we celebrate these sacred rites worthily, O Lord, for each offering of this memorial sacrifice carries on the work of our redemption."

Following the works of the Abbey of Maria Laach, of Dom Ildephonse Herwegen, and especially of Dom Odo Casel, we are only on the track of rediscovering the Fathers and of learning to read and take seriously the texts of the liturgy as being the expression of the faith of the Church. Centuries of incomprehension and advancing disintegration have imposed themselves between our age and that of the Fathers.

Since the Middle Ages, the dynamic aspect of the Eucharistic liturgy—this redemption which "carries on"—if it did not entirely disappear, at least was pushed more and more into the background to give place to the static aspect of the real presence. This was then unilaterally underscored and understood in a most sentimental manner. The "explanations of the Mass" which then multiplied were filled with sentimentally realist explanations of the Mass, explanations based on the idea that the Mass's purpose was to reproduce the passion in a sort of pantomime production, each action representing an action of the passion itself.

It is immediately clear: the Mass became more and more a contemplation of the Lord in his passion only, without any thought for the Resurrection and the parousia, for the glory in which the whole body shares. This admission is of particular interest to us in the context of this study. Unhappily, this is all the truer because this mentality of seeing the Mass only from the viewpoint of the passion has, to a large extent, remained anchored in present-day theology and even more deeply in the spirit of too many priests and of most Christian people.

There was first of all the influence of the Renaissance and of humanism. By artificially resurrecting the mythology of the Graeco-Roman period as a purely literary device, certainly without believing in it, this age was largely responsible for doing away with the biblical atmosphere and "imagery" which the Middle Ages safeguarded, and without which a truly Christian liturgy is not possible. This heritage, along with that violent desire for life which characterized the men of the Renaissance and along with their search for the superhuman (in place of the supernatural), passed on to the age of the Baroque. Not understanding "mystery" at all, even more than the Middle Ages accenting the unilateral insistence on the real presence, and deeply influenced by the ceremonial of the contemporary court, this period succeeded more and more in abandoning the Mass and turned to the salvation of the Blessed Sacrament. They made the liturgy the "etiquette of the Great King," and it was all the more successful, in its conception, the more pompous it was and the less the fascinated crowd understood it.

True, there were reactions and attempts at reform, but these were either cut short or even contributed to the evil's inflammation. There was also that promising attempt in seventeenth-century France, but, unfortunately, it was snuffed out in the battle against Jansenism, the malignancy with which it was unjustly compromised. There were similar attempts in Germany and Austria at the time of the Enlightenment—and we are not lacking in reminders in the recent past that here was the true origin of today's liturgical movement. The intention was good, but it was a misunderstanding of both the liturgical movement and the Enlightenment. With its basic tendencies notably rationalistic and moralistic, it could be interested only in the most exterior aspects of the liturgy, and this only on the level of a simple pedagogic enterprise.

That attempt which Louis Bouyer has called "romantic" restoration [14] failed to go back to the Fathers, and, overshadowed by its admiration for a quite imaginary Middle Ages, succeeded only in regaining the more adulterated "traditional" elements. It succeeded in constructing what might be called false liturgy, just as romanticism succeeded in constructing a false Gothic. Yet it would be unjust to throw out that impulse it successfully begot and which, reëstablished on scientific and thus more sturdy foundations, was among the causes of an authentic renewal. This authentic renewal, "supported" at first by a certain core of people within limited contexts, is more and more on the way to becoming the official concern of the entire Church.

Once we have traced the long road of degradation that the liturgy, in spite of itself, had to travel, it is less surprising to see we have retained, for a long time now, only the "exterior facet of cult, the sensible aspect" of the liturgy. We consider it peculiarly as "a worthy regulation of ceremonies" or as "the totality of laws and prescriptions decreed by the hierarchy in view of the handling of holy rites." The absence of a theology of the liturgy, therefore, cannot be surprising. What theologian would see the

14. *Liturgical Piety*, Notre Dame, 1955. Bouyer has here briefly outlined the history of this evolution.

necessity—even the possibility—of constructing a theology of what appeared to him as "the obligatory ceremonial governing the exterior manifestation of the ecclesiastical cult" (Bouyer)?

In that which has been and still is the outlook of many theologians and the great mass of Christians, the liturgical cycle cannot be the celebration of the fundamental mysteries of the kingdom of God. All we can do is try to rediscover in the liturgical year the historical unfolding of Jesus' life and the examples he gave us during that life; then we can realize as perfectly as possible the ever necessary "imitation of Jesus Christ." As a result, the series of commemorated mysteries takes the appearance of a "slide-show" (an easier expression than "spectacle") which we strive to contemplate. The annunciation, the presentation in the Temple, the entry into Jerusalem on Palm Sunday, the resurrection, and the ascension are placed in the same plane, equally remote from and, on the other hand, equally near us.

Since they have lost the true idea of the liturgical "mystery," pastoral theology and spirituality have tended more and more to contemplate the events of salvation history in the detail of their succession. There is not a doubt that this plumbing of the historical accounts has fortunately taught Christians an intimate love and understanding of the smallest details of Our Lord's earthly life. But it has, at the same time, resulted in a special kind of proximity which totally erases the historical framework and almost makes the past event become present. This is not so only in the innumerable crib-sets up since the Poverello of Assisi, but just as much in the kind of piety it nourishes and in the consequent intimate commerce with the holy personalities.

The paschal mystery will be restored to its rightful place when priests and faithful have rediscovered the sense of "mystery" in the wide perspective which St. Paul opens up in his Letter to the Ephesians (Chapter 1), beginning with God himself and leading to its present realization in the liturgy. Bouyer has stated the case well: at this stage the "mystery is

> . . . the reënactment in, by, and for the Church of the act of Our Lord which accomplished our salvation, that is, his passion and death in the fullness of their final effects—the resurrection, the communication of saving grace to mankind, and the final consummation of all things.[15]

Happily, the Second Vatican Council has provided us with the grand outline of a renewed liturgical theology; it can be found admirably condensed in Articles 5 through 13 of the *Constitution on the Sacred Liturgy*.

3. PREACHING

The lacunae and insufficiencies in the theological teaching just uncovered have had inevitable repercussions in modern preaching. Father Jungmann was perhaps the first to illustrate how the proclamation of the paschal mystery has most often missed the point in our "traditional" sermons. Often influenced by an historical and deistic mentality, preaching offered the mysteries of the faith as isolated past events, unique and already fully realized. God's dynamic, historical interventions, yet beyond space and time, are seldom presented. Specifically, this is true of the central mystery of the Lord's death and resurrection. Mostly, the picture and proclamation is presented of an historical fact, therefore dichotomized, at least partially, from the incomparably more decisive aspect as a present and future salvific reality. Too often, the Easter sermon apologetically "proves" the resurrection; the better sermon, perhaps, hints that the mystery contains the promise of our own resurrection at the end of time—that is, when

15. Bouyer, *ibid.*, p. 18.

it is not content, in the idea so dear to the Enlightenment, to use it as the base for "man's moral resurrection, a thing praiseworthy beyond words."

The true, immediate importance of the paschal victory for our salvation, as the paschal liturgy, which intimately joins the celebration of the paschal mystery with that of baptism, illustrates, has been and is still either presupposed or passed over in silence. However, as Jungmann has said so well:

> The positive thing in the paschal mystery that should be proclaimed is that Christ opened for us the way to a new life, not simply a life freed in justice from sin, but one truly celestial and divine.

And in Article 6 of the *Constitution on the Sacred Liturgy* we read:

> Just as Christ was sent by the Father, so also he sent the apostles, filled with the Holy Spirit. This he did that, by preaching the Gospel to every creature, they might proclaim that the Son of God, by his death and resurrection, has freed us from the power of Satan and from death, and brought us into the kingdom of his Father. His purpose also was that they might accomplish the work of salvation which they had proclaimed, by means of sacrifice and sacraments, around which the entire liturgical life revolves.

Under present conditions, however, we can see why the average Christian fails to see things this way. The teaching on grace has suffered the most by its being dissected from the content of the faith and by its separation from the mystery of Christ. In places we have been able to maintain the link with the mystery of Christ, but without sufficiently understanding the fundamental unity between the passion and the resurrection, the "one" Pasch of the Lord; we see the redemption as the result of the passion, not however of the resurrection. Even here, the positive presentation of the paschal Good News has too often been unduly emasculated.

This phenomenon did not begin only yesterday. The original content of paschal preaching, the Good News of the redemption, began to lose its form towards the end of the fourth century. This coincides with the loss of the ancient form of paschal celebration that saw Easter not as the commemoration of the "day of the resurrection," but as that of the total mystery of the death and resurrection—and thus as the cultural, mysterious celebration of salvation history in its totality. The more effort made to delineate the liturgical cycle and the celebration of feasts as historical days of remembrance, the more the paschal kerygma of the redemption was reserved to Good Friday; the Easter sermon was relegated to being an exposé of the historical event commemorated. Incontestably, this resulted in an impoverishment of the primitive kergyma, the effects of which we still suffer today. Without a doubt, the central content of the feast, the paschal victory of Christ and his people, has lost a major part of its impact.

What we have just said about Easter Sunday sermons is, sad to say, true of sermons in general. Indeed, there are sermons on the redemption, but hardly ever in the paschal perspective. Most often, the only thing preached is liberation from sin, while the positive side of divinization, if not completely ignored, is outrageously pushed aside. Then, too, how rarely we see the redemption presented other than in a shabbily individualistic aspect, with no reference to the ecclesial aspect of the abundant outpouring of salvation economy. There are, to be sure, sermons on saints, many indeed, but they are treated only as models or patrons. When are we going to free them from the moralizing context and present them equally as exemplary realizations of the paschal mystery by men of flesh and bone? As the liturgical constitution says, "By celebrating the passage of these saints from earth to heaven the Church proclaims the paschal mystery achieved in the saints who have suffered and been glorified with Christ" (Art. 104).

Unfortunately, it would be easy to go on multiplying examples of deficiencies in our preaching, grave deficiencies with dangerous consequences. But these are not the worst. As we are going to have occasion to show later, we no longer know what a *homily* is. That is why the paschal mystery, which should appear in every sermon, whether of Sunday or feast day, as present though liturgical and mysterious, now goes practically unproclaimed. But how is it to be known and lived if our preaching, the means par excellence of its proclamation, remains silent?

4. ANTHROPOLOGY

To see some of the causes precipitating the present state of affairs, we should here consider the anthropology, more or less derived from Plato, Plotinus, and Descartes, which underlies theology to so great an extent, pastoral theology and spirituality especially. Then, too, we must remember that we are at least partially the heirs of the Enlightenment's false spiritualism. In a nutshell: if the soul alone counts, if the body is but a "prison" from which to escape as soon as possible, then the soul's happiness suffices. There is no reason whatever to accord any importance to the future resurrection of the body.

The usual presentation of heavenly beatitude has followed a similar line. As the faith teaches, the soul of the just having no faults to expiate enjoys an intuitive, immediate, even facial vision of the divine nature, before the resurrection and the general judgment.[16] Here again, there is in the faith of our people a near

16. See Benedict XII, constitution *Benedictus Deus* (Denzinger, no. 530). This precision was given in dogmatic form in order to end the controversy begun by John XXII who, wrongly basing his supposition on *Revelation* 6, 9, had affirmed the contrary, on his own authority, in several sermons; he eventually retracted this position. (See G. Mollat, *The Popes of Avignon*, New York, 1963.)

total devaluation of the resurrection. Unconsciously, nevertheless really, they ask what the resurrection can add to the beatitude already attained. Clearly, nothing in the Church's doctrine gives credence to such a conclusion. Yet, since the average Christian arrives at it, the reason must be a defective presentation of the total Christian message. If catechesis, preaching, and celebration were clearly centered on the paschal mystery, and if they were, therefore, in some way, at least indirectly, based on biblical anthropology, then the general deficiency we have indicated would not be possible.

In the paschal context, one cannot fail to understand that, "even received into heaven, the souls of the faithful who have died in a state of charity are yet in a state of *waiting;* their fullness will be reached only with the resurrection of the body;" [17] for, as Michael Schmaus has written,

. . . in the state of perfect fulfillment, the celestial life is not just the life of the spirit, but life in a bodily reality. Thus, in its definitive form it presupposes the resurrection of the dead. The intermediary state between the death of the individual and the last day does not yet represent the fullness because, in this state, the spiritual person has arrived at its perfect fullness, yet is deprived of corporeality. In presenting the heavenly life as lived by the elect before the resurrection, we must never silently pass over the fact that the soul is ordained to reunion with the glorified body.[18]

Again, but ever along the same lines, the proclamation of the paschal mystery is also necessary for the teaching of true Christian hope. This is not the individualistic, more or less falsely spiritualistic concept of so many "acts of hope." It is that essentially eschatological, cosmic hope born of the joyously impatient expectation which makes God's people "yearn" for the return of their

17. Conclusions of le Centre de Pastorale Liturgique, Vanves session, collected in *Le mystère de la mort et sa célébration,* p. 457.
18. *Katholische Dogmatik,* vol. 4, Munich, 1959, pp. 219–220.

Lord and thus for full participation in his paschal victory through the resurrection.

This kind of catechesis is possible throughout the liturgical cycle. It is sometimes imposed, as on All Saints' and All Souls' days. A marvelous opportunity, so often neglected, is the funeral, for here the liturgical texts (which demand a homily and instructions) say almost nothing of the soul's fate (with the exception of the orations, perhaps). They all announce the resurrection, not just at Mass, but in the funeral prayers and prayers of burial as well. On All Saints' Day and at funerals, the homily should call to attention the fact that the Church has never had any idea of erasing the words "who rest in the sleep of peace" (remembrance of the faithful departed) from the Mass, even if these words took roots little in conformity with later development of dogma. It seems to us this text rightly permits us to affirm two things: the beatific vision is accorded to the souls of the just immediately; and regardless of the beatitude this vision implies, it is, before the resurrection, only a "sleep" in comparison to what it will be once the whole man is again present.

5. MORAL THEOLOGY. SPIRITUALITY

In moral theology, ascetics, and spirituality, we find the same narrowness of outlook. The paschal mystery (as we treated it above) is, in these areas, almost totally forgotten.

Moral theology, because of its principles—often no more than ethical, because of the concrete, detailed-as-possible conclusions these principles imply—and because it is not always free from the pettiness of unleashed casuistry, has gained such autonomy that often it is hard to draw out its connection with the real heart of Christianity. In the last few years, certainly, there have been fortunate revisions, incontestable progress. Even the better works, however, are literally afraid to abandon the traditional approach, one that makes it ever hard to find the truly decisive place of the paschal mystery.

Ascetics, influenced by a certain voluntarism, the offspring of the Counter-Reformation and by the old, eternally renascent Pelagianism, took as an end in itself the constant pursuit of an "ascetical sports record." Those beautiful gold stars we give our children for their "sacrifices" (spiritual "push-ups," maybe?)—they, of course, show our children what it means to be baptized Christians and implants in them a true understanding of sacrifice.

Spirituality? Take a look at the many "schools" and sub-schools begun by the orders and congregations; each apparently pretending alone to possess the secret of salvation. Now add the "spiritualities" of the secular clergy, that of teaching and hospital religious, that of the young worker, the housewife, the ditch-digger—this is hardly an exaggeration. The logical question, then, in the last analysis, is: Are there not so many kinds of differing Christianities that each demands a special formulation and following out the Christian life? True, our Lord himself said: "In my Father's house there are many mansions." Nobody proposes a uniform conformity spelling the death of spirituality. It is perfectly correct, however, to believe there is but one Christianity, that of Jesus Christ, one basically the same for Benedictine, diocesan priest, and ditch-digger: "There is one body and one Spirit, just as you were called to the one hope that belongs to your call, one Lord, one faith, one baptism, one God and Father of us all, who is above all and through all and in all" (Eph. 4, 4-6). Therefore, before seeking the unity of separated Christians, before concentrating on the legitimate, even necessary, yet accidental differences flowing from the translation of this basically unified Christianity into the practical exigencies of life, is it not primary that Christians be "eager to maintain the unity of the

Spirit in the bond of peace" (Eph. 4, 3) by a spirituality simply Christian, one that cannot be other than Christian?

The question has not been raised whether moral theology, ascetics, and spirituality spring from the center of Christianity, the paschal mystery? If our spirituality continues in the ways it has been taking, a paschal-centered spirituality will not be possible. On this practical level, second only to worship, where Christianity becomes really existential, and ceases to be theory, system, thought, and becomes life in practice—here, in the present situation, the Christian is pulled in all opposite directions. Faith, the sacraments, morality, ascetics, and spirituality seem not only disunified, but even opposed since the inspirations and directives of these areas are so disparate and apparently contradictory. From our point of view, clearly the paschal mystery cannot occupy its central, dominant place in the Christian consciousness because of these defects.

6. PASTORAL "THEOLOGY"

We enclose "theology" in quotation marks because, though all agree that dogma, moral theology, exegesis, and patrology are scientific disciplines, very few would dare say that pastoral theology itself can or should be a science related to theology. Usually, it is seen only as a vague appendix to moral dealing with confessional practice, some good counsels, methods, and "tricks" of success in directing certain organizations. To be convinced of this, one need only glance at the table of contents of the "manuals" of pastoral theology available to the young priest eager to be up on what will, *de facto,* occupy his whole priestly life. Rather than cite examples to justify what we say—a case of beating the obvious—we would rather cover these works with the modest mantle of merciful silence.

In our own seminary days, pastoral theology was something of an appendix to moral theology. Maybe things have changed (we think not), but while we were in the seminary pastoral theology was so much an appendix that the professor, occupied as he was with his moral course, had almost no time to treat it. In practice, all he could suggest was how to make up a card file and use it for house calls. In addition, there was a seminary course on "sex," conducted by a saintly but always blushing director; some homily practice (sermons given in the refectory during meals); and a "course" on catechetics (with *one* practical exercise imposed on the cathedral school children). There was also a course on "liturgy," that is to say, on rubrics; and exactly two hours were devoted to the temporal administration of a parish.

We would like to believe that in today's seminaries, pastoral courses are infinitely better than those we had to suffer through. But are there really very many which go beyond the limits of the so-called "practical"? The same scholar whose survey we mentioned above also reported on this question. We can guess what his answer was.

So, to get back to our point, we can say without any hesitation that, things being the way they are, there is hardly any trace of the paschal mystery in pastoral theology as it is taught today.

7. THE DOUBLE PASCHAL TRIDUUM

We realize—generally but not well enough—the determining influence public worship has on our people's faith, spirituality, and even theological thought at the level of reality. So it is not surprising to find a liturgical factor among the contributing causes relegating the paschal mystery to the periphery in the pastoral ministry.

For St. Augustine, the sacred triduum of death, burial, and resurrection was the center to the liturgical cycle. In his age, the liturgy celebrated the Lord's death, burial, and resurrection in the essential unity that the apostolic preaching had announced to the world. We have already shown how, in the course of past centuries, this fact of capital importance disappeared from the Christian consciousness. In place of the unique triduum, the Church now celebrates a double triduum, and the boundary separating the two cuts the ancient paschal triduum in half. We now have the *triduum sacrum mortis Christi* from Holy Thursday to Holy Saturday, and the *triduum sacrum paschae* beginning on Easter Sunday and lasting until Easter Tuesday inclusive.[19] This is not the language of the rubricists alone, but of the rubrics themselves.[20] In spite of the 1955 reform of Holy Week, we must still use this terminology, for the "traditional" concept has not, for all that, completely disappeared. The unfortunate "demarcation line" continues to break the ancient biblical and liturgical unity of the paschal triduum, with great damage, consequently, to authentic paschal spirituality.

The one paschal triduum slipped into the present double triduum in two stages. The first was that of doubling, beginning in Frankish territory around the year 800, after the paschal celebration was extended over two whole weeks as a single, unified feast. In the countries north of the Alps, agriculture dominated life and Easter fell during the spring sowing time. It was difficult to stop work from Palm Sunday until White Sunday, as was done in Mediterranean lands. It is well to underline the way the change took place.

19. The second triduum, less evident to the faithful, was designated with the rank of a first-class feast attributed to Easter Monday and Tuesday and by obligation of the *missa pro populo* (suppressed by the new *Codex Rubricarum*).

20. If they do not use the terms *"triduum mortis"* and *"triduum paschae,"* they call the *"triduum"* the trinomial: Holy Thursday, Good Friday, and Holy Saturday (rubric at the end of the psalmody of the first nocturn of Holy Thursday). The Sacred Congregation of Rites has used as well the expression *"triduum mortis Christi"* in its decrees (see decree no. 3312).

An impressive collection of documents speaks of a paschal celebration from Easter Sunday to Easter Wednesday inclusive: *Sabbatizandum in Pascha Domini post dominicam tres dies;* from Thursday on, work in the fields was permitted before the daily Mass. It would be wrong to believe that this solution simply reduced the days off work to the minimum. The intent was rather this: to create the rhythm of a double triduum within the ancient and venerable two-week rhythm. The way this was done indeed shows that the nascent Middle Ages were still clearly aware that Easter Sunday looked back to and in some way summed up what preceded it. This explains why, in the adopted solution, the paschal triduum did not begin until Easter Monday. So, in addition to a triduum of the Pasch beginning on Good Friday and extending to Easter Sunday, they celebrated a triduum of the Pasch beginning on Easter Monday and extending to the following Wednesday.

This solution, indeed a good one, prevailed in many places and seems to have been adoped almost everywhere, at least everywhere north of the Alps, by the end of the Middle Ages.

Unfortunately, the second period led to a regrettable mistake. At the end of the Middle Ages, the six days constituting the double triduum were seen as an outline of Genesis and were shifted back a day. They started on Holy Thursday and extended to Easter Tuesday, thus dividing into a triduum of the passion and a triduum of Easter. No longer was Easter the last day of the *paschal* triduum as it had always been, but the first day of the triduum of Easter. Thus the official dislocation of the paschal triduum was effected—and it has not yet been remedied.

There were some ancient precedents for this evolution. Even at Rome, we find very ancient paschal celebrations ending on Easter Tuesday, yet not until the time of the Reformation was this change imposed in a fairly general manner. Then, along with a number of other feasts, Easter Wednesday and the Wednesday after Pentecost were stricken from the list of holy days. A decision of this kind, adopted by the Diet of Ratisbonne in 1542, marks an important step in this evolution which matured exactly one hundred years later, in 1642, when Pope Urban VIII issued his bull *Universa per orbem,* enforcing it for the whole Church. The final evolution had to lead to transforming first Tuesday, then Monday, into work days (in general law; see canon 1247, §1 of *CIC*), although (and in the obligation of *missa pro populo*) these two days retain the same rank as Easter Sunday.

It is not without interest to ask how this damaging second step could happen. Among the contributing factors, there was the profound change in the liturgical role of Holy Thursday. In the primitive Church, this day concluded the forty-days preparation of penitents for reconciliation and prepared for the sacred triduum by the consecration of the holy oils. About this, it is extremely revealing (before the reform of St. Pius X), in contradistinction to Holy Saturday, that the Matins of Holy Thursday were not made up of specially selected psalms, but the usual Thursday ones. True, towards the end of the Middle Ages the other elements of the Office were aligned to the following days of the *biduum passionis* to such an extent that the triad Holy Thursday-Good Friday-Holy Saturday was forced to give the impression of organic unity. The sliding of the celebration of the paschal night to Saturday morning was especially influential in this matter. From the moment one wishes to preserve the ancient veneration of the forty hours Christ spent in the tomb, he is forced to begin on Holy Thursday, which, by that very fact, becomes a day for recalling the passion.

Yet, there is also room to seek elsewhere the basic reason for this evolution. Of a rather sentimental bent, the final age of Gothic succeeded less and less in preserving the ancient and "masculine" unity of Christ's death and resurrection, which even the nascent Middle Ages had understood. Nothing is more significant in this regard than the way of the cross: the most remarkable devotion this age left us does not go beyond the burial of Christ. Four centuries earlier, around the year 1000, when a cycle of diverse details of the passion—along lines the way of the cross would take—was being prepared by order of Othon III for the *Pala d'oro* of the imperial church at Aix-la-Chapelle, it went without saying that it had to begin with Palm Sunday and end with a paschal scene. An age which, to some degree everywhere, knew and fought in vain the abuse of stopping the chant of the Credo after the words "and was buried" was ripe for dichotomizing the day of burial from the day of resurrection!

What went on here and there in the Middle Ages was imposed for all once the Church was faced with the (indeed urgent) problem of reducing the number of feasts. All at once it was clear that there was no convincing motive to justify the celebration of Easter Wednesday. In fact, the ancient paschal triduum had been long forgotten, and, by that very fact, it was quite reasonable to end the paschal celebration on Easter Tuesday.

Is it, then, truly surprising, after centuries of structurally false paschal celebration (a celebration which was and is the principal if not the only source to nourish the faith), that the Christian people—and their pastors with them—are no longer aware of the exact nature of the paschal mystery and of its primary importance?

II.

THE PASCHAL MYSTERY
IN PARISH LIFE

As we have already said, the Christian people's rediscovery of a conscious, joyous paschal Christianity principally concerns the pastoral ministry, deficient in the past and so also in the present. For the reasons just outlined, instead of making the paschal mystery its living focal point, the ministry has pushed it out to the periphery.

So the question: How should we act on the practical plane so that the pastoral ministry may again best fulfill its mission? But this is a poor starting point. Rather, we should take a good look at the ministry to see how far it does go, actually, in fulfilling the paschal mystery; state what it *is* before saying what it must become. Therefore we will be brief, since in a later chapter on the practice of the ministry we will again take up most of the points brought out here.

In a preliminary outline, we may say of the pastoral ministry what Durrwell said of the apostles and the sacraments: it is nothing other than the great "means whereby the Easter mystery spreads outwards."[1]

1. *The Resurrection,* p. 301.

1. BUILDING UP THE CHURCH

According to St. Paul, the purpose of the pastoral ministry is, *de facto*, the "building up the body of Christ" (Eph. 4, 12), the Church. Yet from whatever angle we approach it, the Church always appears to be a mystery, essentially paschal in origin and constitution. Again, Durrwell—for reasons to be explained later—demonstrated at some length that the Church is truly paschal "in her birth—in herself—and in her progress." [2] As corroboration, we will limit ourselves here to a rapid survey of the most important biblical "images" of the Church. [3]

(1) The Church is the body of Christ. An "extension" of Christ's body (as it was before Easter) to the limits of all humanity and creation, however, is indeed unthinkable. The incorporation of each baptized person became possible only the moment that, by death and resurrection, this body attained a new mode of existence, one in which the Lord, though retaining a certain bodiliness, yet freed from the confines of time and space, became the spirit (see 2 Cor. 3, 17). [4] The Head of the Church is the paschal Christ: "that you may know . . . the immeasurable greatness of his power in us who believe . . . which he accomplished in Christ when he raised him from the dead . . . ; and he has put all things under his feet and has made him head over all things for the church" (Eph. 1, 18–22).

(2) The Church is the bride. Without a doubt, this is the

2. *Ibid.*, p. 151. See Cerfaux, *The Church in the Theology of St. Paul,* New York and London, 1959.

3. See the *Dogmatic Constitution on the Church* of Vatican II, Chapters I and II.

4. See Romano Guardini, *The Lord,* Chicago and London, 1954, the chapter titled "The New Man," pp. 448 ff., esp. p. 450. See also Durrwell, *The Resurrection,* pp. 202–220.

fundamental mystery of the entire economy of salvation. This mystery was prepared in successive stages from the "type" of Eve to its perfection at Easter. Note the "figures" of all the women named in the Old Testament: Sarah, Rebecca, Judith, Esther. Note especially the figure in the wonderful "image" of Israel, united to Yahweh by the Covenant (Ez. 16)—often an unfaithful spouse, "adulterous," but always loved, always possessing the promise of being, one day, graciously led back to the desert to the time of the first love (Hos. 2). This mystery is perfected at Easter. The new Eve is born from the opened side of the new Adam, and St. John saw the flow of water and blood. He took note of it intentionally: for the Johannine Gospel, these are the two sacraments forming the Church, baptism and the Eucharist. As St. Paul explains: "Christ . . . gave himself up for her, that he might sanctify her, having cleansed her by the washing of water," and: "no man ever hates his own flesh, but nourishes and cherishes it, as Christ does the church" (Eph. 5, 25–26. 29).

This water is also the living water Ezekiel saw flowing from beneath the threshold of the Temple (Ez. 47); it is the Spirit, the paschal gift par excellence whose source is the temple of the Lord's destroyed and resurrected body,[5] the "spiritual rock" (Ex. 17; Is. 48, 21; 1 Cor. 10, 4) struck by the passion. When Jesus implicitly, yet clearly enough, applied these "figures" of the Old Testament to himself, "the Spirit had not been given, because Jesus was not yet glorified" (Jn. 7, 39). But on Easter, "Yahweh breathed into the nostrils of the Church the breath of life" (see Gen. 2, 7). In accord with the New Testament, the writings of the Fathers abound with the same meaning.

Since we will not have another chance to say it, we will do so here: In our pastoral ministry, we should make extensive use of all the Old Testament "figures," New Testament passages just

5. See Durrwell, *The Resurrection,* pp. 78–91.

alluded to, Gospel passages on the appearances of our Lord after his resurrection (in particular, his meeting with Mary Magdalene in the garden, prepared for by the account of the chaste Susanna [Dan. 13; Saturday of the Third Sunday in Lent], and the supper with the apostles whose typology is intimitely connected with that of "nuptials"; see Mt. 22, 1 ff.; 25, 1 ff., and parallels.)

(3) The Church is the temple of God. Prophecy had predicted the construction of a temple of perfect dimensions (Ez. 40–42), upon a Zion lifted above all the mountains (Is. 2, 2), most holy (Ez. 43, 12; 45, 3), ever surrounded by the cloud of Yahweh (Is. 4, 5), to be God's dwelling place forever (Ez. 37, 27). It will receive mysterious riches and from beneath its threshold shall flow a stream to make the desert green and the Dead Sea alive (Ez. 47, 1–12; Jl. 4, 18). In the last days, the temple will rise in the midst of the people as a sign and cause of holiness (Ez. 37, 28).

That the prophecy be fulfilled, the veil of the old Temple had first to be ripped from top to bottom (Mt. 27, 51), thus manifesting the end of the "figure." And especially, our Lord had to raise up on the third day—by his resurrection—the temple of his body destroyed in the passion (see Jn. 2, 20). Then alone could the holy city—as the author of Revelation saw it—be the "new Jerusalem, coming down out of heaven from God, prepared as a bride adorned for her husband" (Rev. 21, 2 ff.). Yet this city is not just the completed city after the Parousia, but also and first of all the Church on earth in the "last days" begun on Easter.[6]

(4) The Church is the people of God. Just as in the "figurative" Pasch (Ex. 14–15), the horde that left Egypt became truly a people only after the "passage" through the Red Sea, so too the new people begin to exist only after they have followed the new Moses in the *transitus* of his Pasch. In reporting the involuntary

6. See Yves Congar, *The Mystery of the Church,* Baltimore and Dublin, 1960, p. 161.

prophecy of Caiaphas: ". . . it is expedient for you that one man should die for the people," St. John explains that "Jesus should die for the nation, and not for the nation only, but to gather into one the children of God who are scattered abroad" (Jn. 11, 49–52). The Fathers in particular were constant in pointing out this paschal origin of God's people of the new and eternal covenant.[7]

So the Church's origin and constitution are paschal. This is a fact of great import to us now. We must add, however, that though the ministry must "build up" the Church, it must ever more realize that this cannot be done by merely human means, whatever they be. Constant renewal of the paschal origin is a necessity. In other words, the Gospel must be proclaimed, and, as we will show later, it is essentially paschal. The Eucharist is especially necessary, too, as well as the other sacraments which effectively and efficaciously make the paschal mystery present.

2. THE CHRISTIAN

We may call the Christian the material the pastoral ministry forms. Indeed, the Christian is an essentially paschal reality. His earthly life is contained from beginning to end between his baptism, immersing him into the death and resurrection of Christ, and his own death, the full realization of Christ's death in the Christian's body—the beginning, at the same time, of the mysterious "three-days'" delay before the dawn of Resurrection. The Christian's whole life follows the rhythm of the weekly Easter, Sunday. He is sustained, cured, deepened by the sacraments, all of which have their source in the paschal mystery. All in some way make this mystery present. Their purpose is to accomplish the "passage" begun at baptism, to lead the Christian

7. See Jean Daniélou, *The Bible and the Liturgy*, Notre Dame, 1956.

into the "promised land" and to full participation in the risen Christ's life and glory.[8] So the Christian's entire life, including its moral aspect, "is seen to be a mystery of death and resurrection, of mortification and vivification."[9] "The Christian is truly the man of Easter and Pentecost."[10]

3. THE GOSPEL. THE FAITH

Among the many pastoral labors, one of the most essential is proclaiming the Gospel to awaken, engage, and deepen the faith.

Again, indeed, the Gospel is essentially the good news of Easter. When it came to replacing Judas, St. Peter declared: "One of these men must become with us a witness to his resurrection" (Acts 1, 22). The book of *Acts,* which gives us this text, is filled with like texts. St. Paul, in his turn, reminds the Corinthians: "I delivered to you as of first importance what I also received, that Christ died for our sins according to the Scriptures, and that he was buried and that he rose again the third day, according to the Scriptures" (1 Cor. 15, 3). These references suffice for our purposes.

It is not surprising, then, that the faith itself be an essentially paschal reality.

The object of faith is not simply God—God in his serene essence, a God standing in motionless prefection—but the God who raises up Christ, the person of God who breaks into our history through the justifying and judgment-giving act of the resurrection, who obliges us to make a decision, and radically changes the course of our destiny. The characteristic title that the

8. See the *Constitution on the Sacred Liturgy,* Article 6.
9. Conclusions of the Vanves session, in *Le mystère de la mort et sa célébration,* p. 456.
10. Congar, *Laity, Church and World,* Baltimore and Dublin, 1961, p. 10.

Apostle applies to God is: "him who raised Jesus our Lord from the dead." "But the words [for Abraham's faith is a prophetic outline of our own], 'it was reckoned to him,' were written not for his sake alone, but for ours also. It will be reckoned to us who believe in him that raised from the dead Jesus our Lord, who was put to death for our trespasses and raised for our justification" (Rom. 4, 23–25). Jesus' resurrection is such an essential object of the faith that "If Christ has not been raised, your faith is futile and you are still in your sins" (1 Cor. 15, 17).

This idea is not St. Paul's only. As Durrwell has pointed out, it is found in one way or another in Acts as well as in the synoptics.

If we leave out the shades of meaning each author supplies, we may conclude that the Christian faith bears upon the redeeming action of God in Christ, an action which culminates in the resurrection.

The faith, secondly, opens man to the paschal mystery and enables him to assimilate it when presented to him by the Apostle and the sacramental rites. The immeasurable greatness of his power (unleashed by Christ's resurrection) is exercised in our regard, towards us who believe (see Eph. 1, 19). ". . . you were buried with him in baptism, in which you were also raised with him through faith in the working of God, who raised him from the dead" (Col. 2, 12). We could go on multiplying texts in which St. Paul attests, not always explicitly, to the role of faith in equivalent terms and the same goes for the fourth Gospel.

Faith has this power of opening man to the mystery of the paschal Christ because it is not merely an intellectual assent but a handing-over of man to God in his total adherence to the risen Christ; it is man's living assent, in his inmost being, to another principle of life.[11]

Somehow, the faith itself is a death and resurrection. True adherence to the dead and risen Christ obliges the believer to renounce his autonomy. All he has as his own appears valueless.

11. Durrwell, *The Resurrection*, p. 332.

He is called to set out on the road of Abraham, "the father of all who believe" (Rom. 4, 11): from a human point of view he is called to abandon everything representing security and "reasonableness," to abandon himself to a promise leading him along a road of pure stupidity. This means imitation of St. Peter's act of abandoning the last security, already quite illusory, of the boat to walk on the waves, in a way placing his feet solely on the word of the Lord (see Mt. 14, 28 ff.). Among the numerous similar texts of St. Paul, one of the most enlightening is Philippians 3, 11.

Faith, therefore, not only opens man to the paschal mystery, but itself belongs to that mystery; it is an effect of the Father's action in glorifying Christ. It is at once cause and effect, creating the contact with the resurrection that it demands. It is numbered both among the means whereby the risen Christ expands, and among the means whereby man assimilates the resurrection.[12]

The balance of the Christian message requires that we at least mention the role the sacrament of faith plays in conjunction with the faith itself. In our context, it is enough to say: this sacrament serves to establish the basically paschal character of the faith and it seems to us sufficiently to fulfill its role.

4. SUNDAY

In the pastoral ministry, the celebration of Sunday occupies a place of primary importance. Sunday is Easter, fully and completely.[13]

It is the day of the resurrection. The Gospels are at one in pointing this out: it took place on "the night of the Sabbath, as the first day of the week began to dawn." [14] This insistence, as

12. Durrwell, *ibid.*, p. 338.
13. See the *Constitution on the Sacred Liturgy*, Articles 102 & 106.
14. Mt. 28, 1; Mk. 16, 1–2; Lk. 24, 1; Jn. 20, 1.

well as the stereotype formula the evangelists employ, seems, indeed, to get across a theological intention: that of giving a foundation for the primitive community's faith in the essentially paschal reality of Sunday.

Sunday is also the day on which, with marked preference, our Lord chose to appear to his own.[15] The Gospels point it out too often to be an accident that on this day: (1) the appearances took place when all the disciples were assembled in the same place;[16] (2) on each occasion the Lord ate the messianic meal with them;[17] and (3) he communicated messianic powers to them.[18]

An ancient tradition held that the ascension, too, took place on Sunday.[19] In the same way, the glorified Lord crowned his paschal work by sending the Spirit on Sunday (see Acts 2, 1 ff.).

Thus, as the Scriptures themselves attest, Sunday is the only Christian "feast" of divine origin. In reporting these historical happenings, these texts undoubtedly reflect the primitive Church's faith. It understood the "theology of Sunday" that our Lord wished to teach by these happenings. In these "last days," on "the Lord's day" (Rev. 1, 10), in the assembly, in the "supper," in the exercise of his powers now entrusted to the Church, the glorified Lord is "in the midst" of his own, no longer physically, but in a new and unprecedented way. And he is present to give them a share in his own paschal mystery, to anticipate with

15. On Easter Sunday to Mary Magdalen (Jn. 20, 11–18), to Peter (Lk. 24, 34), to the disciples on the way to Emmaus (Lk. 24, 15–34), to the apostles, except for Thomas (Jn. 20, 19–23); "eight days later" to the eleven (Jn. 20, 26); and, surely, a week later, to the apostles by the Sea of Galilee (Jn. 21, 3–17). Note that the last apparition, to John, took place on "the Lord's day" (Rev. 1, 10).

16. Lk. 24, 33; Jn. 20, 19; 20, 26; Acts 2, 1.

17. Lk. 24, 30; 24, 41–43; Jn. 21, 9–13; Mk. 16, 14; Acts 1, 4.

18. Sent on their mission and instructed to baptize: Mt. 28, 18–20; Jn. 20, 21; forgiveness of sins: Jn. 20, 22–23; the Eucharist: the meals, reminding one of Lk. 22, 19.

19. *Letter* of Pseudo-Barnabas, 17, 9.

them the eternal life. (That is why they soon came to call Sunday the "eighth day.") Thus Sunday perfectly verifies the definition of the Christian "feast." It is

. . . An epiphany of God, a manifestation of divine power and grace in order to communicate and assure the supernatural life to men who are solicitous to offer their collaboration in celebrating the solemnity.[20]

From the very beginning, the Church understood and celebrated Sunday as the weekly Easter,[21] while it was clearly some time later that she instituted the annual feast of Easter.[22] It then appeared as an especially solemnized Sunday to commemorate the central mystery of Christianity. Following Christ's command: "Do this in memory of me," the Church celebrated the mysterious supper of the Eucharist wherein the separation of the body and blood "announces the death of the Lord," but she did it on the day Christ conquered death. Therefore, as the most ancient formulary we have of the Mass says, Sunday commemorated the death and resurrection of the Lord (Hippolytus of Rome).

All this clearly demonstrates Sunday as the privileged "day" of the celebration of the total paschal mystery. The feasts instituted later, including those of our Lord, though in the Eucharist they possess the fullness of the paschal mystery, always emphasize only one particular facet of the paschal mystery. It seems, therefore, not quite exact to say, for example that

. . . the mysterious fullness of the evangelical liturgy indeed varies according to whether it is the celebration of a great mystery of salvation, a simple Sunday *per annum*, . . . a feast of a saint celebrated with texts from the common, or a votive Mass.[23]

20. Odo Casel, "La notion de jour de fête," in *La Maison-Dieu*, 1 (1945), p. 26.
21. See the *Constitution on the Sacred Liturgy*, Article 6.
22. See Jungmann, *Pastoral Liturgy*, pp. 389–390, where the author cites Hippolytus of Rome.
23. Jungmann, *ibid.*, p. 390.

Even if we could admit this for the others, never could we do so for Sunday. Logically, this is the place to turn the proposal around and affirm definitively that even a feast celebrating a great mystery of salvation can never attain the paschal plenitude of Sunday. Indeed, Sunday celebrates the greatest mystery of salvation, Easter, and celebrates it in its totality. These differences of interpretation, at first view inconsequential, are really of capital importance if only because of the resulting pastoral applications. We will develop this thought later. Theology and history are in accord in saying that, without Sunday, there is no Christianity at all, but with Sunday, even without any feasts, Christianity is preserved in its entirety.

There has, however, never been any dispute about Sunday. In the course of time, the Churches differed with one another on almost everything, Easter in particular. All, however, always and everywhere, kept and still keep Sunday. Sunday has remained in the Church's tradition just as the apostles knew and celebrated it: the sacrament of Easter. As St. Augustine one day had to say, it is basically similar to the Eucharist to which it is indissolubly linked and without which it cannot be what it is—not simply a memorial, but the very reality and presence of Easter.

5. THE LITURGICAL CYCLE

Element by element, the Church develops the paschal mystery (which Sunday, the Lord's day, re-presents each week) throughout the course of the liturgical cycle. She makes use of the annual solar cycle, but replaces, in a way, the cosmic sun with the "Sun of Justice," Jesus Christ, the Saviour and Lord.[24] By unfolding the "mystery" in the natural course of time, the Church "consecrates"

24. See the *Constitution on the Sacred Liturgy,* Article 102.

65

and sacramentalizes the cosmic year, making it the "year of the Lord."

This cycle took form slowly, without any preconceived ideas or determined plan. The unknown Fathers who contributed to it never thought of a "year of the Lord," and would have had even less intent to establish one. At an undeterminable date, but certainly before the end of the apostolic age, some Churches were celebrating the feast of Easter. In time, they realized the necessity of a preparation period. Under very different influences, especially the need to prepare the catechumens for their baptism in the course of the paschal vigil, and before Lent took on its present form, this preparation period passed through various forms and lengths of time in different ages and places. For reasons mostly unknown to us, the paschal feast was somewhat spread out—prior to it in the "sacred triduum of the death, burial, and resurrection," [25] afterwards in the feast of the ascension and the "holy fifty days" (Pentecost) culminating in the feast of Pentecost. A little later came the feasts of Christmas and Epiphany and the related Advent preparing for them. Advent more or less imitated Lent and was clearly influenced by the conferral of baptism in certain Churches on the feast of the Epiphany. The following centuries saw the institution of a number of feasts and the development of the sanctoral cycle, although they did not basically affect the original cycle, practically stabilized as it was by the institution of the feasts of Christmas and Epiphany.

It has seemed necessary to outline, in general terms anyway, the apparently fortuitous formation of the liturgical cycle. Indeed, as we recently heard during a session on priestly studies, no one is authorized to deny the liturgical year its own complete consistency and, therefore, its completely true influence on Sun-

25. St. Augustine, *Epistle 55*, 24.

days and feasts, and more precisely on the meaning of the Gospel pericopes and the homily applying them. The pastoral consequences which follow are clear, particularly in the area of the present study.

Yet even though—like many other elements of Christianity—the liturgical cycle was formed in the above manner, and though the Church herself only slowly and progressively became aware of it,[26] and whatever the influences, often most human, involved in the process, the liturgical cycle owes its formation in the final analysis to the Spirit of God who directs the Church. It exists and it has a content and a meaning.[27]

That content is the paschal mystery which, in its turn, expresses in worship the "mystery of salvation." Indeed, the mystery of salvation embraces Christ's whole life and, through it, the entire economy of salvation. The liturgical mystery must, therefore, evoke the manifestation of the Word of God made man from his birth in the flesh to his glorious return to the right hand of the Father. Again, as St. Paul says, this mystery of Christ is the supreme manifestation and accomplishment of a mystery of salvation which embraces all human history from the creation to the final consummation.[28] Therefore, the liturgy should ritually represent, along with the mysteries of Christ, the entire history of salvation from creation to the parousia. That is what the liturgical cycle does.

If we now look at man's side of the question, we find ourselves in the presence of a sort of law arising from both human psychology and the events of the economy of salvation. According to this law, each man, called to salvation through participation in the "mystery," must in some way relive the historical stages of God's

26. See the truly enlightening pages which Congar has dedicated to the Church's examination of her own life, in his *The Mystery of the Church*, pp. 138–149.

27. See the *Constitution on the Sacred Liturgy*, Articles 102–105.

28. See *ibid.*, Article 102.

people in the old covenant and fashion himself with the various salvific acts of Christ. Again, the liturgical cycle makes this possible.[29]

To make precise and delimit the exact genre and intensity of the presence of Christ in his Church by reason alone is impossible. It comes from the mystery of the union between Christ and the Church which St. Paul attempts to describe in Chapter 5 of Ephesians. In building up and celebrating the liturgical cycle, the Church does not act solely in virtue of the powers Christ committed to her, but in this union which makes her "the very person of Jesus Christ,"[30] and guarantees that the Holy Spirit ever inspires her to act.

She is especially able to do this because the Lord confided to her the Eucharist. In fact, the celebration of the liturgical cycle is possible only thanks to this "memorial" which produces the substantial presense of Christ and his salvific work. Essentially linked to the celebration of the Eucharist, the liturgical year shares in its power to re-present the work of the redemption. Thus is born the *hodie* of the liturgical cycle.

By force of the fact that the Eucharist is the origin of this "today," it is clear—but worth underlining—that the salvific event of our Lord's life which such and such a moment of the liturgical year presents is not at all isolated and detached from the totality of the redeeming mystery. It is not the only thing represented: for example, at Christmas, the mystery of the birth acquires only the *hodie* of the liturgy, and thus the celebration of this feast is not dissected from the paschal summit of Christ's redemptive work. Always, the entire mystery is re-presented and efficacious, even though such and such a feast be more expressive of a particular aspect of its fullness.

For our purpose in particular, this affirmation is of capital

29. See Bouyer, *Liturgical Piety,* pp. 185–199.
30. Pius XII, encyclical *Mystici corporis Christi;* see also the *Constitution on the Sacred Liturgy,* Article 7.

importance, as we will have occasion to see. As for what we have said, it affirms, as we stated in the beginning, that "the entire institution of the liturgical year is only an expansion of the paschal mystery contained in the sacrament of the Eucharistic memorial." [31]

This is true not only, though in a special way, for Sunday and the feasts of our Lord, but equally, though with less depth, for the feasts of saints. We think it particularly useful to underline this fact in regard to the latter, for today we no longer think in the straight line uniting the feasts of the saints to the paschal mystery. One should remember this simply because the essential element of these feasts is the Eucharistic celebration, as well as the fact that these are *per se* "feasts." The Christian feast, properly understood, is inconceivable without a Christological character; this is the measure of its participation in the mystery of the unique paschal "feast." [32]

Therefore, as the *Constitution on the Sacred Liturgy* says,

By celebrating the passage of these saints from earth to heaven the Church proclaims the paschal mystery achieved in the saints who have suffered and been glorified with Christ; she proposes them to the faithful as examples drawing all to the Father through Christ, and through their merits she pleads for God's favors.[33]

Incomplete though it be, this rapid outline of the liturgical cycle imposes one irrefutable conclusion—important to us here—namely, that in its entirety and in all its parts, the year of the Lord is essentially paschal. Or, in the words of Louis Bouyer:

To say that the Easter observances are the center of the ecclesiastical year leaves much untold: they are the center where all the liturgy converges and the spring whence it all flows.[34]

31. Jean Hild, *Dimanche, vie pascale*, Paris, 1949, p. 267.
32. See Jungmann, *Pastoral Liturgy*, pp. 390 ff.
33. See the *Constitution on the Sacred Liturgy*, Article 104.
34. *The Paschal Mystery*, New York and London, 1951, p. xiii.

6. THE EUCHARIST

We have been led to affirm that, in the liturgical cycle as well as for Sundays, the Eucharist is the Christian Easter par excellence.[35]

In the perspective of the economy of salvation, it fulfills the great paschal "prefigurations" of the old dispensation. The prophetic supper of the lamb at the Exodus was celebrated every year thereafter until the day the true Lamb was slain, —at the very hour that Israel, in the Temple, sacrificed the lambs. That very moment, these lambs lost their significance. As for the day our Lord ate "this passover with you before I suffer" (Lk. 22, 15) and the nature of this meal, he undoubtedly wished to place them in this great tradition. There is the "figure" of the manna, as he expressly says in the discourse at Capharnaum (Jn. 6, 58), after alluding to it by the double multiplication of the bread, in "a desert place," [36] as the Gospels note with unanimous and surprising insistence. At the very center of salvation history is the institution which took place on "the night before he died" as the Canon of the Mass recalls, and the institution account clearly shows our Lord giving us the Eucharist as an efficacious "memorial" of his death, resurrection, and consequent redemption. Since then, and throughout the "age of the Church," from the ascension to the parousia, as St. Paul affirms, "as often as you eat this bread and drink the cup, you proclaim the Lord's death until he comes" (1 Cor. 11, 26)—be it clearly understood: for the Apostle, in the basic unity of the paschal mystery, the resurrection is inseparable from the death. St. Athanasius clearly alludes to St. Paul's word in the paraphrase: "Whenever, together, we eat the Lord's flesh and drink his blood, we celebrate the Pasch." [37]

35. See the *Constitution on the Sacred Liturgy,* Article 47.
36. Mt. 14, 15; 15, 33; Mk. 6, 31. 32. 35; 8, 4; Lk. 9, 10–17; St. John emphasized the fact that the Passover was at hand (Jn. 6, 4).
37. St. Athanasius of Alexandria, *Letter 4; PG* 26, 1379.

The Church, for her part, ever recites in the Canon of the Mass: "We your servants, . . . calling to mind the blessed passion of this same Christ, your Son, our Lord, and also his resurrection from the grave, and glorious ascension into heaven." It is also easy to see this paschal note throughout the Ordinary in both prayers and rites. In the Gloria, for instance, the people pray to him "who takes away the sins of the world" and who now "sits at the right hand of the Father," and in the concluding acclamation call him *"holy . . . Lord . . . most high . . .* in the glory of God the Father."

As for the rites, the separation of the body and blood clearly manifests the Lord's death; and the commixtion, although its origin is not in accord with the symbolism with which we are here concerned, can be seen as an "expression" of the resurrection.

We will not even attempt to trace the paschal note through the proper, since that would require a very large volume in itself, though we will take note that the Alleluia, which is sung during a good part of the year, might well be regarded as the paschal victory chant.

The Eucharist, therefore, is always paschal, since it is the substantial presence of the glorious Christ—the Risen One forever carrying the stigmata of his passion—and, with him, that present dynamism making life spring from death, bringing about the passage of the world to the Father. This is the paschal mystery.

The entire Mass is paschal, that is, it reproduces in its structure the plan of the *sacramentum paschale.* It is the memorial of Christ's death, not in this death as an isolated event, but as the culmination point of the redemptive economy: death, resurrection, glorification. *Unde et memores. . . .* The Mass is the sacramental rite of salvation. It is the rite of Easter.[38]

38. Pie Duployé, "Pâque la sainte," in *La Maison-Dieu,* 6 (1946), p. 12.

Without the Eucharist, the pastoral ministry is but a sham, a grand illusion, nothing less than a great fake. Indeed, this is all that we mean to say: the very core of the pastoral ministry is essentially, through and through, paschal.

7. THE SACRAMENTS

The other sacraments, too, in their own way, have this paschal character.[39]

They are germinally contained in the Eucharist because it contains our Saviour's passion; they are but complementary aspects of the victory it won.[40]

All of them, with the Eucharist and baptism, flowed from our Lord's opened side.[41] The Church herself takes note of this paschal origin of baptism, confirmation, Orders, and the sacrament of the sick by blessing the holy oils for their administration in the Mass of the Holy Oils. She gives Orders only during Mass, and the usual place of the nuptial blessing is during Mass.[42] As for the sacrament of penance, at least in ancient times, the Church administered it under the form of exclusion from and readmission to the Eucharist.

(A) Baptism

Liturgical tradition and ancient discipline are firm in emphasizing the paschal character of baptism, in intimately relating it to the celebration of Easter. In fact, during the second century, the

39. See the *Constitution on the Sacred Liturgy*, Article 61.
40. *The Paschal Mystery*, p. xiii. Bouyer quotes in this connection St. Thomas Aquinas, *Summa Theologica*, III, q. 73, a. 5, ad 2; and q. 62, a. 5.
41. See Jn. 19, 34.
42. On the nuptial blessing, see *Codex Rubricarum*, n. 381.

celebration of baptism was reserved for Sunday, the weekly Easter, and progressively to the annual feast of Easter. Since then it was conferred only by immersion—a practice clearly based on a text of St. Paul that we will cite later—baptism was indeed seen as the "antitype of Christ's passion," as St. Cyril says so well.[43]

After the sixth century, the custom changed, for those to be baptized in the now Christian world were practically all children. Prudence recommended a change *quam primum*. But the Church, throughout the paschal vigil office (even when it was anticipated the morning of Holy Saturday), continued to proclaim the baptismal catechesis of the "prophecies," and to bless the baptismal water. Also, the liturgical books have invariably kept some very significant rubrics. The ritual prescribes, at least in the baptism of adults, that as often as possible baptism be reserved to the paschal vigil.[44] The missal prescribes a final catechesis to the catechumens before or during the "prophecies" of Holy Saturday,[45] and the bishops' ceremonial forbids, except in necessity, the administration of baptism from the First Sunday of the Passion to Holy Saturday inclusive.[46] Since the restoration of the paschal vigil, baptism has been surely provided for [47]—when it cannot be had in small parishes, we immediately sense something essential lacking in the celebration; the congregation solemnly renews the renunciation of Satan and the baptismal profession of faith.

The Church's constant liturgical tradition is itself sufficient proof of the paschal character of baptism. But there is more. In the perspective of the economy of salvation, baptism fulfills an

43. *PG* 33, 1081; quoted by Jean Daniélou, *The Bible and the Liturgy*, p. 43.
44. *Rituale Romanum*, Tit. II, Cap. 1, n. 41.
45. *Missale Romanum*, rubric after the *Exultet* and before the prophecies.
46. *Ceremoniale Episcoporum*, Lib. II, Cap. 27, n. 18.
47. The redacation of this rubric is rather an unfortunate one: instead of presenting baptism as normal and obligatory, it is content with using the ancient formula that speaks of possibility.

array of Old Testament "figures" which the paschal vigil "proph-ecies" and the Preface for the blessing of the water recall. Indeed, most of these "types" are by nature paschal, for example the passage through the Red Sea. There is no theme more alluded to in patristic tradition because the Fathers annually constructed their baptismal catechesis on these "images." [48]

We also have the formal testimony of Scripture. St. Paul in particular is constantly underlining baptism as the Christian's immersion into the Lord's paschal mystery:

Do you not know that all of us who have been baptized into Christ Jesus were baptized into his death? We were buried therefore with him by baptism into death, so that as Christ was raised from the dead by the glory of the Father, we too might walk in newness of life (Rom. 6, 3–4).

Or again:

. . . and you were buried with him in baptism, in which you were also raised with him (Col. 2, 12; see also Eph. 2, 4–6; Col. 3, 1–4).[49]

(B) Confirmation

We do not have such numerous and formal Scripture texts for the sacrament of confirmation. This, however, does not imply the sacrament to be other than profoundly connected with the Lord's Pasch.

This is obvious in the solemn rite of administration. The bishop signs the candidate with the sign of the cross, annointing him with holy chrism. The sign of the cross clearly evokes the glorious passion of our Lord, and the holy chrism, blessed as it was in the Mass of the holy oils on Holy Thursday, in its turn

48. See Jean Daniélou, *The Bible and the Liturgy*, pp. 60 ff.
49. See the *Constitution on the Sacred Liturgy*, Article 6.

establishes the paschal connections with this sacrament. Daniélou has shown how, for confirmation too, the Fathers constantly saw the fulfillment of the "figures" of the old covenant.[50] In this regard, he particularly cites a text from St. Ambrose magnificently explaining the paschal meaning of the signing and annointing:

> The Father has marked you with the seal, Christ the Lord has strengthened you, and he has put into your heart the pledge of the Spirit. Receive also something more. For, as the Spirit is in your heart, so Christ is in your heart. You have this in the Song: "Set me as a seal upon your heart" (8, 6). You, therefore, have been marked by the imprint of his cross, the imprint of his passion. You have received the seal in his image that you may live in his image.[51]

Passion, resurrection, therefore: Easter.

Then, too, along with baptism and the Eucharist, confirmation has always been considered one of the three sacraments of initiation. In antiquity, it was administered immediately after baptism. The venerable Oriental Churches still preserve this custom. The present law of the Latin Church fixes the normal age for confirmation at seven years (except in danger of death). However, historically confirmation is the second step of Christian initiation, after baptism, and should be received before the Eucharist. We have reason to hope that this hierarchy will once again be observed, for as the *Constitution on the Sacred Liturgy* declares:

> The rite of confirmation is to be revised and the intimate connection which this sacrament has with the whole of Christian initiation is to be more clearly set forth; for this reason it is fitting for candidates to renew their baptismal promises just before they are confirmed. [Article 71]

The normal place for confirmation, then, is between baptism and the Eucharist. These three sacraments together form a unity. Yet baptism and the Eucharist are sacraments of the paschal

---

50. *The Bible and the Liturgy,* pp. 114 ff.
51. St. Ambrose, *De Sacramentis,* VI, 5–7; quoted by Daniélou, *ibid.*

mystery. It would be more than surprising were the sacrament of confirmation completely different.

This results, again, from the very significance of this sacrament. The word "confirmation" comes from the Latin *"firmare,"* meaning "to strengthen." Certainly, the Christian is strengthened by confirmation, but more so and first of all it is the baptism itself which is "confirmed." If baptism, then, plunges the Christian into the death and resurrection of the Lord, the sacrament which strengthens it must also be paschal.

This is also true in its effects. Confirmation is a new outpouring of the Spirit, completing and deepening that of baptism. Yet the Spirit is the "fruit" of Easter. By this very fact, confirmation is of its nature paschal since it confers the fullness of the paschal mystery on the Christian.

Finally, there is a certain correlation between Christ's baptism and the subsequent descent of the Holy Spirit on one hand, and the Christian's baptism and confirmation on the other. St. Cyril of Jerusalem, for example, has shown in his baptismal catechesis that the Christian, configured in Christ in his death and resurrection by baptism, is configured in him in confirmation since he is the Anointed One of God anointed by the Spirit. Christ's baptism followed by the descent of the Spirit is the "figure" of his death and initiation as *Kyrios.* The double sacrament of baptism and confirmation brings about the Christian's participation in the Lord's royal death and exaltation. This parallel once more establishes the paschal character of confirmation.[52]

(C) Penance

Once again, the Church's ancient discipline is such that it lets us put our finger on the paschal essence of penance. In fact, from

52. On the body of doctrine, see M. Bohen, *Confirmation,* New York, 1963.

the time she began the practice called "public penance," she made it a masterpiece of preparation for the paschal mystery celebration. The penitents were "excommunicated" on Ash Wednesday and reconciled on Holy Thursday. The Lenten liturgy was occupied almost as much with the penitents as with the catechumens, and even today the ferial Masses bear this witness. The Holy Thursday reconciliation applied the paschal redemption to the repentant sinners and permitted them to participate again, by communion, in the mystery of Easter.

This discipline has disappeared, but the exclusion and reconciliation of sinners ever have their place in the pontifical. It has retained a rubric requiring the bishop to remind his priests in synod of their duty to invite the faithful to confession at the beginning of Lent.

Taking a term dear to the Fathers, the Council of Trent called penance the "laborious baptism." [53] Although very different from baptism, as the fathers of Trent took note, penance is related to it—as this name implies—and is, therefore, like it, paschal in nature.

Seen in the perspective of the economy of salvation, sin is a "return to Egypt"; and its pardon, a new paschal liberation. In the parable of the prodigal son (Lk. 15, 11–32), we clearly can see a description of the sacrament of penance in it essentials. In "the best robe" the father tells them to "fetch quickly" in order to clothe his contrite, already forgiven son, we can see an allusion to the white robe of baptism, the white robe penance restores.

Actually, in both baptism and penance, our consciences are cleansed "from dead works" in the blood of the Lord (see Heb. 9, 14). This is the "blood of the covenant, which is poured out for many for the forgiveness of sins" (Mt. 26, 28).[54] In other

53. Session XIV, Chapter 2; Denzinger, no. 895.
54. See Jn. 1, 29; Rom. 3, 25–26; Col. 2, 13–14; 1 Jn. 2, 2; 4, 10; 1 Pet. 1, 18–19; 3, 18; Rev. 1, 5. 7. 14; 22, 14. See also A. G. Mortimort, *The Signs of the New Covenant,* Collegeville, 1963, pp. 220 ff.

words, as St. Thomas Aquinas has said, in the sacrament of penance Our Lord's passion is at work.[55]

Then, too, our Lord was himself careful solemnly to underline the bond linking Easter and the sacrament of penance when he instituted the latter the very night of his resurrection: "On the evening of that day, the first day of the week, . . . Jesus came and stood among them and . . . said to them, 'Receive the Holy Spirit. If you forgive the sins of any, they are forgiven; if you retain the sins of any, they are retained' " (Jn. 20, 19. 22–23).

We will note this express communication of the Spirit to the Church, doubtlessly alluding to St. Peter's words (Acts 2, 38), confessed in her liturgy: "he himself is the forgiveness of all sins." [56] And, as we must repeat, the Spirit is the great "fruit" of Easter!

(D) *The Anointing of the Sick*

There is a profound relationship between this sacrament and those of baptism and penance. Its purpose, in fact, is to bring to perfection the paschal victory over Satan (whose "kingdom" is manifested by sickness as well as by death), the victory begun in baptism and restored in penance. As the prayer in the anointing of the sick says:

In the name of the Father, and of the Son, and of the Holy Spirit. May any power that the devil has over you be utterly destroyed, as I place my hands on you, and call upon the help of the glorious and holy Mother of God, . . .

This anointing always affects the health of the soul, begun by baptism and restored by penance, and sometimes that of the body. And it remits sin, as the prayers continue:

55. *Summa Theologica*, III, q. 84, a. 5.
56. Post-Communion of Tuesday after Pentecost.

May the Lord forgive you by this holy anointing and his most loving mercy whatever sins you have committed by the use of your sight [hearing, etc.].

Yet, as we have just seen, the remission of sins is essentially a paschal work.

The frequently repeated signs of the cross and the oil blessed in the Holy Thursday Mass of the holy oils manifest, liturgically, the basically paschal character of the anointing of the sick.

At the end of an evolution that we can only call unfortunate,[57] this sacrament, primitively a sacrament specifically intended for the sick, became above all "extreme unction," the dread sacrament of the dying. This expresses one of its real facets, but we must hope that the Church will, on the one hand, make this again a true sacrament of the sick, and on the other hand, give us a different formula for the dying. Regarding the former matter, the *Constitution on the Sacred Liturgy* reads:

"Extreme unction," which may also and more fittingly be called "anointing of the sick," is not a sacrament for those only who are at the point of death. Hence, as soon as any one of the faithful begins to be in danger of death from sickness or old age, the fitting time for him to receive this sacrament has certainly already arrived. [Article 73]

In itself, however, the sacrament of the sick is also the sacrament of the dying:

In relation to the final combat, it plays a role analogous to that of the pre-baptismal signings and anointings. It marks the faithful with the seal of Christ and thus removes him from danger, all the while strengthening him for the supreme victory.[58]

The sacrament, therefore, helps the dying Christian fully to bring about the Lord's Easter in the passover of his own death, to

57. See Bernhard Poschmann, *Penance and the Anointing of the Sick,* New York, 1964, pp. 234 ff.
58. Jean Hild, "La mort, mystère chrétien," in *Le mystère de la mort et sa célébration,* p. 241.

make it an act of adoration and of worship—in a way, it is the last, most fully participated in of all the "Masses" of his life. It is, at the same time, his dedication to the life of glory,[59] that is, to the heavenly fullness of the paschal mystery.

When the anointing is really the sacrament of the dying, it forms a unit with the apostolic benediction and the recommendation of souls.[60] The apostolic benediction at least retains this prayer:

> May our Lord Jesus Christ, the Son of the living God . . . give you back that robe of grace which was first given to you in baptism.

As for the recommendation, it sounds a magnificently paschal note, illustrating all the essential aspects of baptism.

(E) Orders

An extensive demonstration of the paschal nature of Orders is not necessary. Instituted on Holy Thursday in the course of the last supper in order visibly to perpetuate the One High Priest's priesthood, essentially at work in his paschal sacrifice, this sacrament is especially related to the Eucharist, the sacrament of Easter, and the other sacraments, all paschal in character. Its duty is "building up the body of Christ," the Church, a mystery entirely paschal in origin and constitution.

(F) Marriage and Virginity

The paschal mystery is a nuptial mystery. Easter fulfilled the almost innumerable "figures" and prophecies in some way form-

---

59. St. Thomas Aquinas, *Comm. in Sent.,* IV, d. 23, a. 2.
60. *Rituale Romanum,* Tit. V, Cap. 6 & 7.

ing a theme throughout all Scripture, clearly announcing redemption as nothing other than the "marriage" of God with humanity. From the opened heart of the new Adam on the cross, the Church, the new Eve, was born, and there all redemption was granted: not just the forgiveness of sins, but at the same time the share in divine life and glory, the uniting of "the children of God who are scattered abroad" (Jn. 11, 52) who, one day, will sit at the "marriage of the Lamb" (Rev. 19, 7).

The sacrament of marriage is rooted in this mystery—"a great mystery" (Eph. 5, 32). The mission of marriage is to re-present, to actualize the mystery of Christ and the Church, and somehow to be its revelation.

And so, marriage is a mystery of death. There is no love without sacrifice: "Husbands, love your wives, just as Christ also loved the Church, and delivered himself up for her"—to the cross! (Eph. 5, 25). But, just as much and even more, it is a sacrament of resurrection and life, for its mission is to give life to the children of men and, at the same time, the children of God, heirs of the kingdom.

Marriage has this power because it is, as St. Robert Bellarmine says,

. . . a sacrament like the Eucharist not only at the moment of its celebration, but throughout the time it endures. As long as the spouses live, their society is ever the sacrament of Christ and the Church.[61]

For this reason, the spouses are "mediators of grace"[62] for one another. They have the power and responsibility of mutual sanctification. But every grace and all holiness comes from Easter. And, to use a term dear to the Fathers, their community is an *ecclesiola,* a cell of the Church,

---

61. *De Controversiis,* III, IV; quoted by Pius XI in his encyclical *Casti Connubii.*
62. Pius XI in *Casti Connubii.*

not only in the sense of cells germinating to increase, but also in the sense of living cells in which the life and mystery of the whole body exist in an elementary way . . .[63]

The family, then, is a "miniature" of that Church which is paschal through and through. Thus, in its *Constitution on the Sacred Liturgy,* the Church declared that the rite of marriage "is normally to be celebrated within the Mass." [64]

8. THE SACRAMENTALS

It is no exaggeration to say that the sacramentals, too, have a paschal aspect, but once again this needs to be said in context. If the sacraments, properly so called, operate *ex opere operantis Christi,* the sacramentals operate *ex opere operantis Ecclesiae.* In other words, their effectiveness reaches far beyond the merits and dispositions of the subject. In fact, their origin, like that of the sacraments, but somewhat differently, is to be found in the living union of Christ and his Church, an origin which is, therefore, paschal.

In this perspective, the sacramentals the Church uses to surround the Eucharist itself are on the top rung—almost everything except the account of the institution—as are those, too, surrounding the other sacraments to make their celebration as human as possible and their effects comprehensible. Thus, flowing as they do from the sacraments, these sacramentals must evidently participate as well in their paschal character.

Aside from this first category—but ever in the context of the unique ecclesial liturgy—there runs a whole gamut of sacramentals from various benedictions of the ritual to blessed objects such

63. Yves Congar, *Lay People in the Church,* New York and London, 1965, p. 202.
64. *Constitution on the Sacred Liturgy,* Article 78.

as holy water, medals, etc. Seen from Roguet's viewpoint, the benedictions of the ritual especially, and the objects blessed in an evidently much less solemn way, extend the rays of the Eucharist to all creation, thus witnessing to the cosmic dimensions of the paschal mystery.

It seems proper here briefly to mention a hierarchy of processions, sacramentals extending from those which, within the Mass, are in a way privileged, to those taking place by themselves—such as the processions of palms, rogation days, Corpus Christi, the Assumption, marriages, funerals, pilgrimages, and so forth. All, indeed, are in some way signs of God's people coming out of the Egypt of this sinful world. In baptism they make their passage through the true Red Sea, already a paschal people, yet ever "strangers and pilgrims" in the world where they have no "lasting dwelling," for they are en route to the final passage of the Jordan, the general judgment, to the promised land and the heavenly Jerusalem. The march is victorious, triumphal, from Easter to Easter, to its manifest and final fulfillment.

9. PRAISE

As we have already said, though this people on the march is yet in the "exile" of this world, by participating in the paschal mystery they nonetheless belong to the kingdom already begun. They have a "down payment" in it, a share in its life. From Easter to Easter—all the Easters, the feast itself and every Sunday, every Mass and every sacrament—they travel the ascending spiral of the liturgical cycle every "year of the Lord," as a group and as individuals, progressively ascending the mountain of God until that "Day," reaching the unknown summit, they find themselves face to face with their Lord coming in majesty for the final consummation.

As they sing in the "figurative" liturgical processions, God's people, throughout the march, cannot but chant the hymn of the redeemed; the "song of the Lamb":

> Great and wonderful are thy deeds,
> O Lord God the Almighty!
> Just and true are thy ways,
> O King of the ages!
> Who shall not fear and glorify thy name, O Lord?
> For thou alone art holy.
> All nations shall come and worship thee,
> for thy judgments have been revealed.
> [Rev. 15, 3–4]

This takes place in the eucharistic celebration and the other sacraments as well. These are not only the "just and straight ways," the effects of the paschal mystery coming to her, but also the elements of the worship the Church offers to God.

This worship continues in the sacramentals. Our processions across the fields in the raw poetry of morning, sun, and dew, and all the blessings—these too are intended, in both meaning and purpose, to assign fields, automobiles, food, and all things their place in the magnificent procession of creation returning to God. They gather the note of each dew drop, adapting it to the score of the grand symphony of mounting adoration—"through our Lord Jesus Christ"—transfigured and divinized by him, to the "Father of light."

Aside from some late exceptions, every oration in the Roman liturgy thus ends by lifting our attention towards him who, in his transfigured humanity, is our Head, our advocate with the Father: we make every prayer rise before the throne of God "through Jesus Christ, your Son, our Lord, who lives and reigns with you." This "through our Lord" runs from the beginning of the liturgical prayer to its end, and is, in a way, its basic law, not only at Easter or the ascension, but throughout the year. Easter always dominates the Church's prayer.[65]

This constant praise—"They ought always to pray and not lose heart," our Lord said (Lk. 18, 1)—the Church sings in the Divine Office. In it she takes note of all the hours of the day, of the weeks and the years, clothing them in the psalms and great canticles of Scripture to "offer up a sacrifice of praise to God, that is, the fruit of lips that acknowledge his name" (Heb. 13, 15). She does this also in that indissoluble union uniting her with Christ who, in her and through her, continues the song of praise begun "in the time of her exile on earth," the song resounding forever in the heavens—in the Spirit who "helps us in our weakness; for we do not know how to pray as we ought, but the Spirit himself intercedes for us with sighs too deep for words" (Rom. 8, 26).[66]

All this praise—that of the sacraments, of nature "consecrated" by the sacramentals, of the Office—is united in the Eucharist to be sublimated in the perfect—paschal—sacrifice, in the "thanksgiving" our Lord offered, once for all, to the Father, never ceasing to represent it so that humanity and creation may ever be associated in it.

Thus

. . . all Christian worship is but a continuous celebration of Easter: the sun, rising and setting daily, leave in its wake an uninterrupted series of Eucharists; every Mass that is celebrated prolongs the Pasch. Every day of the liturgical year and, within each day, every instant of the sleepless life of the Church, continues and renews the Pasch that our Lord had desired with such great desire to eat with his disciples while awaiting the Pasch he should eat in his kingdom, the Pasch to be prolonged for all eternity. The annual Pasch, which we are constantly recalling or anticipating, preserves us ever in the sentiment of the early Christians,

65. See Jungmann, *Pastoral Liturgy*, p. 414.
66. See the *Constitution on the Sacred Liturgy*, Article 83.

who exclaimed, looking to the past, "The Lord is risen indeed," and turning towards the future, "Come, Lord Jesus! Come! Make no delay." [67]

At the end of these reflections on the Church's "sacramental system," once again we face the obvious and clear conclusion: the entire liturgy—the very life of the Church—is paschal, completely, totally.

If Easter is *the* Christian feast, the entirety of Christian worship will be paschal and will have no other objective than to expand the many potencies of the paschal mystery and ensure its efficacious presence so long as the Church is engaged in the life of history and of the world. Thus it will be the medium and perpetual point of contact between the time of the world and the time of the Lord.[68]

10. MORAL LIFE. ASCETICS. SPIRITUALITY

The pastoral ministry, again, is the pastor conducting his flock along the ways of the moral life, teaching them an ascetic, giving them a spirituality. The numerous New Testament texts uniting essential Christianity to a truly existential context continue to repeat, one way or another, that morality, ascetics, and spirituality have but one aim and goal: to translate the fundamental mystery of Christian existence into concrete Christian life, that is, to maintain, continue, deepen, and perfect the paschal mystery into which baptism has assumed the Christian; fully to actualize, through constant recourse to worship and the sacraments, our Lord's death and resurrection germinally shared in through the sacrament of regeneration: "the grace of this sacrament which they have received," as the Church says in her Easter liturgy.

67. Louis Bouyer, *The Paschal Mystery,* p. xiii.
68. Dalmais, "Le 'mystère,' Introduction à la théologie de la liturgie," in *La Maison-Dieu,* 14 (1948), p. 82.

Since baptism immerses the new Christian in Christ's death, this death should be rendered effective throughout the entire exercise of the Christian life, which thus is seen in its entirety as a mystery of death and resurrection, of mortification and vivification.[69]

This is the perspective our understanding of the Lord's words demands:

If any man would come after me, let him deny himself and take up his cross daily and follow me. For whoever would save his life will lose it; and whoever loses his life for my sake, he will save it. [Lk. 9, 23 f.] [70]

As a disciple and, even more, as a member of Christ, the Christian must "imitate" and "follow" him who "emptied himself, taking the form of a servant . . . humbled himself, and became obedient unto death, even death on a cross," so that with him, God also may exalt him (see Phil. 2, 7 ff.).

St. Paul especially constantly bases morality, ascetics, and spirituality on the Christian's paschal nature:

How can we who died to sin still live in it? Do you not know that all of us who have been baptized into Christ Jesus were baptized into his death? We were buried therefore with him by baptism into death, so that as Christ was raised from the dead by the glory of the Father, we too might walk in newness of life. For if we have been united with him in a death like his, we shall certainly be united with him in a resurrection like his. [Rom. 6, 2–5]

Most of the moral teaching in the Pauline epistles, especially those to the Churches in Colossae and Galatia, is built entirely on this foundation:

If then you have been raised with Christ, seek the things that are above, where Christ is, seated at the right hand of God. Set your minds on things that are above, not on things that are on earth. For you have

69. Conclusions of the Vanves session, in Le mystère de la mort et sa célébration, pp. 455–456.
70. See also Mt. 16, 24–27; 10, 38–39; 10, 23; Mk. 8, 34; Lk. 14, 27; 12, 9; 17, 33; Jn. 12, 25–26.

died, and your life is hid wih Christ in God. [Col. 3, 1–3; reading of the paschal vigil]

The case of incest in Corinth that St. Paul takes up has given us the beautiful text which the Church proclaims on Easter morning:

Do you not know that a little leaven leavens the whole lump? Cleanse out the old leaven that you may be a new lump, as you really are unleavened. For Christ, our paschal lamb, has been sacrificed. Let us, therefore, celebrate the festival, not with the old leaven, the leaven of malice and evil, but with the unleavened bread of sincerity and truth. [1 Cor. 5, 6–8]

There is also St. Paul's response to those who thought themselves authorized by his own words:

"All things are lawful for me," but not all things are helpful. "All things are lawful for me," but I will not be enslaved by anything. "Food is meant for the stomach and the stomach for food"—and God will destroy both one and the other. The body is not meant for immortality, but for the Lord, and the Lord for the body. And God raised the Lord and will also raise us up by his power. Do you not know that your bodies are members of Christ? Shall I therefore take the members of Christ and make them members of a prostitute? Never! [1. Cor. 6, 12–15]

In fact, once the Christian has, through baptism, entered into a mystical and objective relation with the dead and risen Lord, thus leaving the sphere of death (that is, of *sarx,* sin, and the Law) in order to enter the sphere of Christ to the point of being transferred into a "new life," of being "in Christ," a member of Christ's body and a "new creature," he must necessarily actualize this sacramental state in his moral life. In innumerable variations, without ever tiring of it, the Apostle repeats this dogma of Christian existence: Become what you are! "So you also must consider yourselves dead to sin and alive to God in Christ Jesus"

(Rom. 6, 11). It is not enough to possess the new life, we also must "walk in newness of life" (Rom. 6, 4); we have no right to be content with having received the Spirit, we must also "live by the Spirit" (Gal. 5, 25), be "led by the Spirit" (Rom. 8, 14). Whoever has been delivered from the slavery of sin and has thus become a "slave of God" must put himself entirely at his service (see Rom. 6, 17).

We could thus compose a ledger; on one side would be the Apostle's texts attesting to what has been given, and on the other that yet to be done.[71]

"We know that our old self was crucified with him so that the sinful body might be destroyed" (Rom. 6, 6)—but: "Put off your old nature which belongs to your former manner of life" (Eph. 4, 22; see Col. 3, 9).

"And those who belong to Christ Jesus have crucified the flesh with its passions and desires" (Gal. 5, 24)—but: "Put to death therefore what is earthly in you" (Col. 3, 5); "if by the Spirit you put to death the deeds of the body you will live" (Rom. 8, 13).

"But you are not in the flesh" (Rom. 8, 9)—but: "Let not sin therefore reign in your mortal bodies, to make you obey their passions" (Rom. 6, 12; see 13, 14b).

"For as many of you as were baptized into Christ have put on Christ" (Gal. 3, 27)—but: "But put on the Lord Jesus Christ" (Rom. 13, 14).

"Therefore, if any one is in Christ, he is a new creation; the old has passed away, behold, the new has come" (2 Cor. 5, 17)—but: "put on the new nature, created after the likeness of God in true righteousness and holiness" (Eph. 4, 24; see Col. 3, 10).

"Christ is in you" (Rom. 8, 10); "it is no longer I who live, but Christ who lives in me" (Gal. 2, 20; see Phil. 1, 21; Col. 1,

71. See Alfred Wikenhauser, *Pauline Mysticism,* New York, 1960, pp. 149 ff.

27)—but: "that Christ may dwell in your hearts through faith" (Eph. 3, 17).

Some try to see these so apparently opposite "indicatives" and "imperatives" as nothing but contradictions. But this is not so. In reality, they are but an expression of the tension between the very really given "life in Christ" and the concrete life rooted in the "flesh" and sin, realities that have not lost all their power. The Apostle knew this tension only too well from his own experience (see Rom. 7, 21–25), and from that which he encountered every day in his communities. For him, the sacrament had established the foundation of the new life, and, as a result, man was removed from the sphere of sin and of the "flesh"; but for all that, the Christian is not a morally perfect person. On the contrary, he must translate what he has been given objectively into his moral life, must make it real.

To do this, a restrictive ascetics is needed to "put to death . . . what is earthly in you: immorality, impurity, passion, evil desire, and covetousness, which is idolatry" (Col. 3, 5 ff.). This mortification is absolutely necessary: "for if you live according to the flesh you will die, but if by the Spirit you put to death the deeds of the body you will live" (Rom. 8, 13).

And there must be a positive asceticism to help forward the thrust of the Spirit, to bring human nature, weighed down with the flesh, into step with the Spirit: "that we also may walk in newness of life" (Rom. 6, 4). "So run that you may obtain the prize" (1 Cor. 9, 24).[72]

The insistence with which St. Paul underscores the role of the Spirit in this "mortification" itself shows well that he is not pushing "ascetics for ascetic's sake." This must be a Christian ascetic, a death "with Christ." It must, therefore, be a paschal ascetics, not a simple exterior "imitation" of our Lord's sufferings

72. Durrwell, *The Resurrection,* p. 339; see the section "Christian Effort," pp. 338–342.

and death, but one lived in communion with Christ glorified who is the source of the Spirit "poured into our hearts" (Rom. 5, 5).

This does not mean any loss of life for no reason whatever, but rather "for my sake" (Mt. 16, 25). The purely exterior ascetical works the Pharisees practiced with a zeal worthy of a greater cause, which they wished to impose on his disciples, these he rejected, opposing to them the primacy of interior worship (see Mt. 9, 13; 12, 7). St. Paul did not hesitate to follow in this same tradition battling against the Judaizers who sought to impose circumcision, abstentions, and the observance of days, months, and seasons on the faithful (Gal., *passim;* Col. 2, 16 ff.), like the deceitful spirits "who forbid marriage and enjoin abstinence from foods which God created to be received with thanksgiving" (1 Tim. 4, 3). For him, this all amounted to a pure and simple denial of the paschal mystery into which the faithful were immersed:

> If with Christ you died to the elemental spirits of the universe, why do you live as if you still belonged to the world? Why do you submit to regulations, "Do not handle, Do not taste, Do not touch" (Col. 2:20). If then you have been raised with Christ, seek the things that are above (Col. 3, 1).

Such an ascetics possesses nothing of true humility; this "worship" is "puffed up without reason" (Col. 2, 18). The liberty acquired in Christ is compromised and one falls back under the dominion of the law (Gal. 4, 21), the elements of the world (Gal. 4, 9; Col. 2, 8), and the angelic powers (Col. 2, 18). In this way, one is "not holding fast to the Head" (Col. 2, 19). On the contrary: "Are you so foolish? Having begun with the Spirit, are you now ending with the flesh?" (Gal. 3, 3).

Christian ascetics, Christian spirituality, and—we may say—Christian mysticism are what the Apostle himself practiced:

> Indeed I count everything as loss because of the surpassing worth of knowing Christ Jesus my Lord. For his sake I have suffered the loss of

all things, and count them as refuse, in order that I may gain Christ and be found in him, not having a righteousness of my own, based on law, but that which is through faith in Christ, the righteousness from God that depends on faith; that I may know him and the power of his resurrection, and may share his sufferings, becoming like him in his death, that if possible I may attain the resurrection from the dead. [Phil. 3, 8–11]

This essentially paschal character of concretely lived Christianity is found in a most striking manner in the new commandment. Our Lord gave it in the very context of his Pasch, in close conjunction with the paschal sacrament of the Eucharist (Jn. 13, 34). His intention is clear. Before all, the measure of fraternal charity is not the love a man has for himself (Lk. 10, 27; see Lev. 19, 18), but the love with which the Lord loves his own "to the end" (Jn. 13, 1), in the very moment of his Pasch.

The new commandment proves how really a "new creation" is brought about in the Christian by the paschal mystery. In fact, it takes man so much against the grain that Christ can truly impose it only on those into whose hearts the charity of God is "poured into our hearts through the Holy Spirit which has been given to us" (Rom. 5, 5)—and given on Easter. If "by this all men will know that you are my disciples" (Jn. 13, 35), is it not because in our charity we manifest our paschal being?

St. Paul will have to remind the Corinthians of the deep bond linking the new commandment to the paschal sacrament of the Eucharist. Their reunions where "each one takes first his own supper, and one is hungry," jar with "the Lord's Supper." To eat this bread and drink the Lord's cup while lacking charity is the "unworthy communion," and an answer will be demanded (see 1 Cor. 11, 17 ff.), for thus is the paschal mystery, present and efficacious in both the Eucharist and charity—in a different manner, of course—betrayed, and its unity broken.

There can be no doubt, then, according to the New Testament, that morality, ascetics, and spirituality—and mysticism—are necessarily of the same nature as the mystery they are called to translate into the Christian's concrete life. In a certain sense, they themselves are part of this mystery—which is essentially paschal.

The purpose of this chapter has been to state the place the paschal mystery does in fact, objectively, occupy in the totality of the pastoral ministry. To do this, you might say, we have "taken it apart" to examine it piece by piece in its essential elements. For those who would make the necessary distinction between the domain and technique of the pastoral ministry (in itself still secondary despite its vast extent and extreme variety) and these essential elements of pastoral theology itself, who would see these last as they are given by revelation itself, the result of this quest cannot but be deeply impressive. The place of the paschal mystery in the pastoral ministry? Objectively, it is penetrated with it in all its parts; even better, it is filled to the brim with it!

May we be permitted to underline, in passing, the point that, in this perspective, the paschal mystery is seen as a marvelous fulcrum of unity. Instead of having the justly lamented disorder so harmful to Christian life,[73] by putting the paschal mystery in its Christianity. Faith, sacraments, morality, ascetics, spirituality, and mysticism all converge on it. In this vision of things, there can no longer be a gap or any opposition: faith, sacraments, and moral life are on the same level, are one in prolonging the other, and demand a continual interaction.

We have indeed said it: objectively, this is the place of the paschal mystery in the pastoral ministry. The point? It should have this same place in the minds of pastors and in their daily pastoral practice.

73. A dispersion exemplified in numerous catechisms that place side by side, without any connection between one and the other, such things as truths that we must believe, commandments to be kept, means of salvation.

III.

THE RENEWAL OF THE PASTORAL MINISTRY

As we have seen above, multiple causes, some serious, have led pastors to push the paschal mystery practically to the periphery of their pastoral activity. Obviously, this condition will not be changed by a few measures in the matter of practical details. Rather, we must attack the basic causes engendering this situation and then establish the basic conditions making possible a pastoral ministry centered on the paschal mystery.

1. AN APPEAL TO THEOLOGIANS

First, this implies an insistent demand upon theologians, exegetes, and professors of universities and seminaries. Nothing can be done unless they elaborate and transmit a theology itself united about the paschal mystery. This demand comes not from the understandable but somewhat naïve enthusiasm of the neophyte who has just discovered the primary importance of this mystery. Rather is it raised by the statements of a theologian of the rank of Karl Rahner.

Clearly, this demand is not leveled solely and strictly at dogmatic theologians. We have just as much need, to mention but a few examples, of the truly Christian anthropology we demand especially of the exegetes; of a moral theology more Christian than that which we generally possess; of a real pastoral theology as we have already had occasion to say; of a theology of the liturgy; and so forth.

It would be foolish to have illusions about this; it will be a long-term effort. Then too, it is always difficult to break from the categories consecrated by centuries of "tradition," and it involves certain risks which not many are disposed to run. What, therefore, is to be done now?

The Church fulfills her mission especially and principally in the "care of souls." Yet, in fact, the Church's mission is the same as that of Christ himself. The Lord founded the kingdom of God and thus brought about humanity's salvation. Thus we must say the same for the Church. She is at the service of the kingdom and the salvation of men, a mission fulfilled by announcing the word, celebrating the sacraments, and ordering her whole ecclesial life.

These are the same three "means" which Christ himself named: "Go therefore and make disciples of all nations, baptizing them in the name of the Father and of the Son and of the Holy Spirit, teaching them to observe all that I have commanded you . . ." (Mt. 28, 19–20).

This is precisely what Pius XII says in *Mediator Dei:*

Mediator between God and men and High Priest who has gone before us into heaven, Jesus the Son of God . . . was not content, while he dwelt with us on earth, merely to give notice that redemption had begun, and to proclaim the long-awaited kingdom of God, but gave himself besides in prayer and sacrifice to the task of saving souls, even to the point of offering himself, as he hung from the cross, a victim unspotted unto God, to purify our conscience of dead works, to serve the living God.

In obedience, therefore, to the Founder's behest, the Church prolongs the priestly mission of Jesus Christ *mainly* through the sacred liturgy. She does this first at the altar, where constantly the sacrifice of the Cross is re-presented and, with a single difference in the manner of its offering, renewed. She does it next by means of the sacraments, those special channels through which men are made partakers in the supernatural life. She does it finally by offering to God, all good and great, the daily tribute of her prayer of praise.

We are, therefore, dealing here with a definitively, uniquely divine work—not with a human work, not even a work of those whom the Lord has sent. He has not given them the mission to accomplish what he alone can do, but only that of being what they are able to be: "stewards of the mysteries of God" (1 Cor. 4, 1; see Tit. 1, 7; 1 Pet. 4, 10), "fellow workers for God" (1 Cor. 3, 9). It would be well to keep re-reading Chapter 3 of 1 Corinthians: "What then is Apollos? What is Paul? Servants through whom you believed, as the Lord assigned to each. I planted, Apollos watered, *but God gave the growth*" (3, 5 ff.). And so, in stating that the growth—natural as well as spiritual—cannot be attributed to human activity, but uniquely, solely to divine action, St. Paul is only restating—and a different image—what our Lord himself gave the apostles to understand when he sent them to "preach the kingdom of God and to heal the sick": "Take nothing for your journey, neither staff, nor wallet, nor bread, nor money; neither have two tunics . . ." (Lk. 9, 1 ff.; see Mt. 10, 9–14; Mk. 6, 7–13). The route that he had them take is that of grace, and not just because of what they are to bear, but because they themselves are to count on grace alone, and, for the most part, to renounce all human means.[1]

What we have just said permits us to say first what the pastoral ministry is not, or rather what it should never be. It is not a "psychological activity," nor an art of religious education, nor an enterprise of human persuasion. This seems so evident, yet how often in practice does the pastoral ministry retreat to this level?

Men, the Church's members, do not decide when the kingdom will be established, do not invent their own means to transmit

1. See Joseph Dillersberger, *The Gospel of Saint Luke*, Westminster, 1958, in particular Book III, on "The Acceptable Year" in Galilee, pp. 245 ff.

the redemption and choose when the kingdom will be established. Our Lord's response the day of the ascension is, *mutatis mutandis,* valid for all apostles and for all time: "It is not for you to know the times or dates which the Father has fixed by his own authority; but you shall receive power *when* the Holy Spirit comes upon you, and you shall be witnesses for me," meaning, we think, by the power of the Holy Spirit, not by yourselves and by your happy inventions (see Acts 1, 7 ff.). "For my thoughts are not your thoughts, neither are your ways my ways, says the Lord. For as the heavens are higher than the earth, so are my ways higher than your ways and my thoughts than your thoughts" (Is. 55, 8). And the "figure" of Gideon remains ever valid: "lest Israel vaunt themselves against me, saying, 'My own hand has delivered me'" (Jgs. 7, 2). Along this same line, St. Paul recalls what Moses had already said: "I will have mercy on whom I have mercy, and I will show pity on whom I will show pity." And he comments: "So it depends not upon man's will or exertion, but upon God's mercy" (Rom. 9, 16). We might add, for such seems to be Paul's thought: in *his* ways and with *his* means.

It bears repeating: the practical pastoral ministry is not a human invention, a human organization; it is not an activity of purely human origin. It cannot be established like a parish or disocesan secretariat. The laws of "publicity" and "propaganda" are not its tools. The sources of the pastoral ministry are essentially and primarily theological.[2]

The indications given above also permit—and oblige—us to delimit the proper domain of the pastoral ministry. Its field is what concerns the coming of the kingdom—which is to come *into* the world progressively, but which is not *of* this world (Jn. 18, 36)—and the salvation of men. Anything outside this is not its concern, or only most indirectly. But we must yet come to an understanding of what the kingdom is and what it is not. Too

2. De Coninck, S.J., "Les orientations actuelles de la théologie pastoral," in *Nouvelle Revue Théologique,* 2 (1954), p. 138.

often we are inclined to include nearly everything: social institutions, the family, even civilization itself.

In the first place, then, the character of the pastoral ministry is instrumental. It collaborates in the building up of the spiritual temple of "living stones," but God is the real builder. It plants and waters, but God gives the increase. In a word, it is essentially sacramental, although in very differing degrees. Its action culminates in the sacraments properly so called, especially in baptism and the Eucharist which communicate and deepen "life," and in penance which restores it.[3]

Let it be well understood: this is not a question of reducing the pastoral ministry to the celebration of worship and the administration of the sacraments. The proclamation of the word, in varied and multiple forms, plays a capital role here. Also, the pastoral ministry always has intimate ties with, for example, spiritual direction, the organization of Catholic action, the evangelization of unbelievers, and so forth. This is what we have felt obliged to underline: all these aspects of the pastoral ministry, not directly sacramental, to be authentic must somehow proceed from the "mystery" participated in through word and the sacrament, and in addition, must consciously and effectively have it as the unique goal to which they lead. The pastoral ministry is and always will be composed of the things just mentioned and more, but, in the last analysis, always to make men's contact with Christ as successful as possible. Yet this contact normally and essentially takes place in the sacraments. In other words, and to return to St. Paul's usage: in the organization of Catholic action, in the evangelization of unbelievers, the pastoral ministry plants and waters.

3. "One thing of incalculable importance, though somewhat ignored for the past forty years, has been brought to the fore in some recent works, namely, that the constitution of the mystical body and the realization of its unity are, in St. Paul, dependent on a sacramental action. Faith is the ground on which we are justified and on which we grow as members of Christ through acts that are animated by a living faith; but it is baptism that incorporates us in him, and the Eucharist that makes us all a single body, his body." Congar, in *The Mystery of the Church*, pp. 73–74.

God, in the sacraments, can give the increase (see 1 Cor. 3, 6).[4]

It is not at all a question of excluding from the ministry the means and laws regulating the conduct of men in the natural order—inasmuch as these means and laws can be reconciled with its ends and spirit, but the pastoral ministry cannot be reduced to them. In fact, in the exact measure that these purely human means play the predominate role, pastoral effort departs further and further from its true end. Every pastor knows how many fortuitous, purely peripheral things can be points of encounter and sometimes form the "bridges" of successful pastoral contact. But when possibilities of this sort arise, we must never forget that the contact thus established is yet on this side of the true threshold and, in the same measure, it is yet far from the heart of its goal. Human means are legitimate only insofar as and as long as they are understood and used as "bridges" leading to that heart.

There is often some pertinent, but exaggerated, insistence on the role the pastor's "personality" plays in the ministry. It is exaggerated because the same does not hold true for a pastor and a military leader. Really, the pastor's action does not at all correspond to the force of his personality—this is both his consolation and his suffering. The more his action approaches the center—the center is Christ—the more his personality loses its importance, all the more clearly does it take on the aspect of an instrument, a sign by and through which the Lord himself personally acts. Certainly, how the pastor knows he is an instrument and sign has its importance, but this "how" changes nothing that interests us in this context.

It is thus apparent that the sacraments, which incontestably are the summit of the entire ministry, are at the same time eminently

4. This conception of the pastoral ministry has been confirmed by the *Constitution on the Sacred Liturgy* and by the *Instruction on the Liturgy* of the Sacred Congregation of Rites. See Articles 9 and 10 of the constitution, and Article 5 of the instruction.

liturgical actions. The Eucharist, the core of all worship, is simultaneously the summit and fulfillment of the entire pastoral ministry. Just as in Christ's earthly life, the downward movement from the Father to men and the upward movement from earth and men towards the Father compenetrated each other and finally became but one, so it is for the essential acts of the Church's life wherein the Lord's priestly work continues. In the life of the Church, praise for God and "peace" for men are but one. As the Church says more than once in her liturgy, this is an *admirabile commercium*.[5]

Now seems to us the time to underscore another characteristic of the ministry. It is indeed the care of souls, but not primarily as occupation with individuals or even with a great number of "souls"; most importantly, it is at the service of all: its mission is to "build up the body of Christ." It is here called to collaborate in making its own the way willed by God wherein the individual is not saved as an individual but as a member of a people. The individual's redemption is a function of his incorporation into Christ. The final end of redemption consists in all men, through Christ and in the unity of the Spirit, being one with the Father and one among themselves. This takes place in the ecclesial community and even more precisely in the parish. The individual receives life, and that life is maintained in him by the fact that he is a member of that community whose head is Christ and whose soul is the Holy Spirit. When a bishop entrusts a parish to a pastor, he is not so much charging him with the "care" of a certain number of souls; primarily, he makes him responsible for the community. He makes him "the faithful and prudent steward whom the master will set over his household to give them their ration of grain in due time."[6] The pastor's mission, then, is

5. See, for example, the Secrets of the Tenth and Eleventh Sundays after Pentecost.
6. See Lk. 12, 42—antiphon of the Communion in the Common of Doctors.

essentially to care for Christ's body, to protect it, to nourish it, to heal it, and this in the very territory to which the Church has sent him. Let us mention in passing: this is where we see the difference between the task of the pastor and that of the university or youth-group chaplain. One is charged with a whole, the body; the other with a greater or lesser number of individuals. We can draw an analogy to this in the evolution now taking place in the medical profession. There is always the classic doctor, specialist or not, who settles somewhere waiting for the sick to come and consult him or to call him to their homes, having, then, to treat individual "cases." Alongside these "traditional" doctors, there is an increase in "company doctors," for example, who also are occupied with individual cases, but whose specific responsibility is the preventative medical surveillance of the personnel, of working conditions and hygiene, in order to maintain the good health of the personnel. Their primary role is not to be occupied with those sick or injured among their charges, but to watch over working conditions, atmosphere, hygiene, and security in the enterprise.

Obviously, the comparison is quite imperfect. The pastor's relationship with his parish is much more profound and vaster. But, even abstracting from the term of comparison, from looking at the whole thing, the analogy should be advantageous in reminding pastors that they have not only to cure the "patients," but also to break the bread for those in good health. This will contribute much to ridding the ministry of a certain hospital atmosphere which only chokes the Christians who are less in need of "cures" than of substantial food. The point of view the pastor should take is that of the parish community; and his actions, whether positive or negative, will be determined by what benefits or harms that community.

All this means that the pastor's mission cannot be reduced to a task of conservation and healing, but, positively, it primarily consists in leading the parish to itself fulfill its own role, to be, in this precise place on earth, the living Church and thus to fulfill here and now the Church's very mission. The parish community, not the pastor, is the Church. He is but a member invested with precise functions. Yet the Church's noblest and most essential mission is the glorification of the Father and the adoration of the Most Holy Trinity. Our Lord's words, "My house shall be a house of prayer" (Lk. 19, 46; see Is. 56, 7), are as valid and more valid for the spiritual temple of the parish community than they were for the edifice which was its image. Parish life will attain its greatest accomplishment, its center, and its end when the "holy people" of the parish, assembled for the "breaking of the bread" and the "supper of the Lord," "proclaim the death of the Lord until he come" and, in so doing, with Christ, offer Christ to the Father in "the sacrifice of praise." All the other tasks confided to the parish have their place concentrically about this summit or lead to it as so many degrees.

Once again, the most certain—and the simplest—theological facts give evidence of the profound relationship inseparably uniting the liturgy and the pastoral ministry one to the other. Whatever the particular situations of a parish, its most pressing needs of whatever nature, every pastor's most important and urgent task is to awaken his parish to the authentic celebration of the divine worship and to make them capable of it. This supposes appropriate instruction, the education of interior and exterior attitudes, and practical exercises. In many a place it will even be necessary to recreate the sense of community, patiently to overcome the individualism of those who—and they are legion—seek in worship only the "satisfaction of their religious needs," measure the value of a celebration by the "spiritual profit" they receive from it, and feel, there especially, the need "to be for self."

There is a special need for understanding the Sunday worship as "service of God" which, as such, imposes on the individual the duty of aiding his parish to fulfill this "service." As a cell of the Church, the parish is seen entrusted here and now with the mysteries of Christ, and it has in itself and in each of its members the duty of worthily celebrating them in the feasts and in the seasons of the liturgical cycle. As the Church's essential mission, worship requires the pastoral ministry to lead the parish to "worship the Father in spirit and truth" (Jn. 4, 23).

In doing this, the pastoral ministry finds its own fulfillment. Man acquires health and holiness in adoration, and the redemption is applied to him and realized in him through participation in Christ's mysteries re-presented in the course of the liturgical cycle.

The pastoral ministry and the liturgy are not identical. But though the distinction is necessary, this very distinction, if properly made, manifests a mutual compenetration on the level of the sacramental and communitarian character of the ministry so that, if one should live at the expense of the other, both would have to face the unhappy consequences. One cannot disappear without both disappearing. They have an absolute need for one another, and they make incessant demands upon one another. That means that the interests of the liturgy can never be in contradiction with the interests of the pastoral ministry. Moreover, what is true liturgically is true pastorally, and vice versa.

From what we have thus been able to suggest about the pastoral ministry, must we not conclude that it should be essentially *one?* Too often we tend to speak of such things as the liturgical mission, the mission to the aged, to vacation camps, to the scrupulous, and so forth. This dissipation of the ministry into every type and name is serious. By "specializing" the ministry we run the definite risk of destroying it. There cannot be a ministry of this alongside a ministry of that. There is but one ministry.

What we have attempted to outline is the Church's incessant effort to fulfill her mission, the direct continuation of Christ's mission. The instrumental, that is to say, the sacramental ministry transmitting and realizing the redemption is the paschal mystery.

And this is a ministry in which the "liturgical ministry" does not stand beside an ensemble of other "ministries," even if this "liturgical ministry" is considered the noblest and most important of all. Further, the entirety of the one ministry proceeds from its source, the only possible source, the Word and the sacraments, in which and through which God communicates his salvation, in which the entirety of the unique ministry returns to the liturgy (in the broad sense of the word) as to its sole aim the glory of the Father.

2. PASTORAL THEOLOGY

Since we spoke above about the deficiencies in the pastoral ministry, and at the same time about the necessity of forming a right concept of it, there is no point in discussing at length why the elaboration of a pastoral theology is an urgent task. We need a theology, that is, along with dogmatic or moral theology, a tract on the Church based on revelation—not simply a synthesis of numerous accounts of pastoral experiences; for as De Coninck has said so well, "pastoral technology is but a house built on sand." [7]

A true pastoral ministry presupposes a theology of the Church. Much remains to be done in this field, but, since the encyclical *Mystici Corporis,* the essential note has been given: we are called on to see in the Church a living entity, and not just a juridical one, an organism not to be confused with an organization. The Second Vatican Council has now given us precise directives on this matter: in its *Dogmatic Constitution on the Church* it provides the essential elements for a theology of the priesthood, in other words, of a theology of the hierarchy and its role; in the same constitution, it provides the principles for a working out of a

7. *Art. cit.,* p. 137.

105

theology of the laity. It also provides for those conditions indispensable for the construction of a sound and authentic pastoral ministry.

As we have said before following De Coninck, the sources of pastoral science are "essentially and primarily theological."

In the first place is Scripture. This is the place to note how the Master himself went about establishing the basis of the Church. Exegetical work ought to take stock not only of the Lord's words and commands, but of his attitudes as well: his incomparable example of the "shepherd" (Jn. 10), the way in which he corresponded to the mission the Father had given him (see Jn. 20, 21), his manner of acting in the formation of the apostles, in the apostolate to the crowds, to individuals. Acts lets us see how the first disciples and the apostles understood this pastoral lesson given by our Lord himself, and how they put it into practice in the beginnings of the building up of the Church. The letters, those of St. Peter and St. Paul especially, but those too of St. John, St. James, and St. Jude, furnish decisive indications.

Tradition allows us better to understand what Scripture tells us. That is to say, the magisterium, in all its forms, is in its turn the source of pastoral theology. In elaborating it, there will be place to note the papal consensus on this point, as well as the decisions of councils and synods, pontifical and episcopal directives.

In its own way, Church history, the writings and lives of great pastors of the past, sheds light on the pastoral ministry. In noting, for example, the influences which marked a St. Charles Borromeo, whose life was so important for the entire episcopate, and in thus discovering certain constants, we can better understand that the pastoral ministry is not an individual and passing charismatic activity, but the very life of the Church—even better: the life of the supreme Pastor who continues to watch over and protect his people.

So then, in the order of descending importance, Scripture,

tradition, and Church history constitute the essential sources of pastoral theology. Alongside them come the auxiliary sources such as religious sociology, medico-pastoral treatises, and many another discipline.

A pastoral theology so constructed cannot but have the paschal mystery at its center.

Yet there is always the condition that one bring to his elaboration all the probity and rigor which every scientific work requires. Seeing how this is often done, we have reason to underline this primary and indispensable condition.

We are thinking in particular of how pontifical directives are utilized. By situating all of them indistinctly on a plane, by passing over their context, and by altering them a little, one can make them say almost anything he wishes. Thus, by grouping together only the warnings in *Mediator Dei*—in their most authentic context—one can most easily succeed in constructing a radical condemnation of the liturgical movement. Yet what has followed has shown that, though these reservations were indeed intentional, the positive passages were more important to Pius XII; the revolutionary reforms which followed witness this.

A good method is to make a close "critique" of scriptural texts before using them for a theological construction. It is, then, no lack of respect or obedience to do the same with pontifical texts. Thus, and in the very first place, they must be classed according to their "literary genre": whether a decision of dogmatic import such as Pius XII's constitution *Sacramentum Ordinis,* an encyclical, an allocution on a particular occasion, or something said in a private audience. There is a difference. Also, it seems indispensable to us to distinguish between a reflection of the Church's authentic tradition and what the treatment of a given situation or the preoccupations of a particular era may be.

But then, we think it right to ask: Is it correct to cite such a passage from Pius XII's allocution to the Assisi congress, one clearly envisioning the universal Church as such, to show that "the liturgy is not at all the pastoral ministry"—true in itself—in a context dealing explicitly with the concrete ministry, that is, parish? This example is not at all imaginary, but, for understandable reasons, we abstain from giving the reference. . . . Then, too, in the area of the relationships between parish and diocese, to which we will return, must we not use prudence since the relationships between episcopate and priesthood have not been entirely clarified?

The most exacting scientific rigor is especially necessary in the use of auxiliary sources. This puts us on grounds totally distinct from revelation. There can never be a question, for example, of attributing equal importance to the findings of religious sociology and the content of Scripture and tradition.

Allow us a final remark regarding this question of method. Aside from certain diocesan aspects, sometimes even universal aspects, the pastoral ministry is exercised practically, primarily on the parish level. Pastoral theology, therefore, should always be concentrated here, more precisely, on the level of the *normal parish,* which should not, if possible, exceed five thousand members. Presently, it is true, we have some Gargantuan parishes in our cities too large for men to care for. This is a fact, but not an authorization to impose views conformed to the needs of these overextended, unformed parishes, or to refuse solutions impractical on their level. Yet these are the parishes we hear of the most. The solution is not to conform pastoral theology to them, but to break them up into normal-sized parishes, a difficult but not impossible job. It will be expensive—but funds always turn up for enterprises we really want to undertake.

It should be clear by now, although we think there is a need to expose certain exaggerations, that we have no intention whatever of going to the opposite extreme. We have already said: there are pastoral aspects that can be solved only on the diocesan level, even, in certain limited cases, on the level of the universal Church. Though, for example, the parish may be equipped to form Catholic action militants, it is not equipped to form their directors: for this latter, the framework of the diocese is necessary, or at least that of a group of parishes. But more. Presently, a good number of parishes do not measure up to the needs of the Christian life, partly because they are too big, partly for other reasons too complex and numerous for us to analyze here. According to all the evidence, parishes must, on one hand, be multiplied where necessary, and on the other, must look for new pastoral adaptations. Despite the boldness entailed, if necessary they must break the parish mold, even the most accepted of customs.

In so defending the institution of the parish, we feel we are in line with Paul VI in his June, 1963, allocution to Rome's clergy, the day after his election:

[The Pope] certainly is not unmindful of life's different milieus nor that the parish cannot do everything by itself; he is not unmindful of the laity whose action and influence are indispensable for the expansion of God's kingdom; but at the same time he wishes to insist on the ancient and venerable parish institution, the fundamental community of the Christian people. It is the center of the liturgical life where faith is communicated and preserved and, finally, from which charitable works radiate.

One would be less in danger of getting off the track were he to remain on the grounds of a sound *parish theology*. For there is a parish theology and of a different authenticity than the pseudo-theologies of games, of costume, and of the thousand other things some are amused to invent. There is a parish theology in the full sense of the word because, at least indirectly, God revealed and Christ instituted the parish. This is a fact because a theological relationship exists between the parish and the Church, a relationship stemming not from the fact of the Church's authoritative creation of the parish, but from the parish as the actual representative of the Church.

In fact, inasmuch as the Church is an "event," it is necessarily a local community. As an "institution," the Church clearly preëxists the parish. But no one will deny that wherever the Church acts, that is, teaches, confesses the faith, and celebrates the Eucharist, she acquires a degree of actualization superior to what she possesses in her permanent existence alone.

In herself, she is a visible society, but to be really and concretely visible, the Church needs to actualize her tangible, historical, spatial, and temporal reality through the action of men of flesh and bone. She must, therefore, become an "event." Not that these "events" create her existence always and each time anew, but they bring her from a certain potentiality to a certain actuality. Again, in becoming an "event" as the "communion of saints," that is, as a society, the Church becomes more fully an actual perceptible "event" in time and space.

This takes place especially in the celebration of the Eucharist. In fact, in her very essence, the Church is the continued presence in the world of the Word of God made man. Thus, indeed, is she "event" in the most actual and intense of manners in this act wherein the crucified and risen Lord is substantially present, communicating salvation; an event, at the same time, where the unity of Christians with Christ and each other concretizes itself most tangibly and visibly in the Eucharistic banquet. By the very fact that the Eucharistic celebration sacramentally anticipates the banquet of the eternal marriage feast, it announces the definitive form of the Church, since it sacramentally contains its origin: the sacrifice of the cross.

But, of its nature, the Church's celebration of this sacramental act of worship is necessarily local: the Eucharist can be celebrated only by a community gathered in one place. Without, for all that, denying the Church's universal mission and her relationship to all humanity, we must nevertheless affirm that in her very essence the Church is constituted in view of local concretization. As a local event, the Eucharist does not have just a place in the Church; the Church herself can become completely a local "event" only in the Eucharistic celebration. On the basis of these facts, we can see how the Church can call by the name *"ecclesia"* both the local community and the grand communion of believers throughout the world.

Far from being a sort of "agency" of the universal Church, created afterwards, and which the Church did not have to institute, the parish is the "event" of the universal Church herself. The local community is not the result of an atomization of the universal Church; it is much rather the Church in its greatest actuality.

True, the Eucharist can be celebrated by communities other than the parish: monastic communities, youth groups, and so forth. In these local celebrations, too, the Church becomes an "event." But by right and in fact, the parish community is the primary, most normal, and most spontaneous form of the local community because it is the most natural, the one born of life itself and not, as the others, of more or less artificial formations. Thus it would be false to limit the actualization of the Church to the parish community, but it is no less true that the Church is especially and before all "realized" in the parish.[8]

3. THE ORGANIZATION OF DIOCESES

This reordering of theology should find translation, concretely, on the level of diocesan organization as well. At present, there are generally several "diocesan commissions" in our dioceses: Catholic action, social action, charities, C.C.D., etc., supervised by temporarily assigned priests and, sometimes, permanent laymen. Besides these, when all goes well, there is a poor "Liturgical Commission" or an "Office of Pastoral Liturgy" composed of pastors, professors, or chaplains trying their best to do something alongside their principal functions.

8. See Karl Rahner, "Theology of the Parish," in *The Parish,* edited by Hugo Rahner, Westminister, 1958, pp. 23 ff.

This is the state of affairs. To declare it is not at all an irreverent criticism. Anybody who knows something of the history of our dioceses realizes that these organizations were born of needs felt one after another. Commissions and offices, therefore, were not created in the abstract by some bureau, but originated from the very movement of diocesan life and authentic pastoral needs.

This positive aspect does not prevent in such an organization—or perhaps better, disorganization—the translation, indeed not intentional but nonetheless real, of an idea of the pastoral ministry in which the paschal mystery, source and unity of all pastoral ministry, takes exactly the same insignificant place given it at the parish level.

Despite the cooperative good will animating commissions and offices, by the absence of a common inspiration and thus a common organization, by the force of circumstances (without reproach to anyone), each of these commissions occupies its own little corner, in dispersed order, and not always with the greatest of inter-unity. Often inspired by national organizations, they are frequently in danger of losing sight of the diocese or particular region. Thus, even when these inconveniences are reduced to the minimum, the diocesan ministry and, consequently, the parish ministry cannot have the unity we have shown to be so imperative.

Allow a comparison. The bishop is the source of the entire ministry; he is *the* pastor. In the present organization, the bishop is: the head of social action, the "servant" of charity, the celebrant of pastoral liturgy, the teacher of Christian education. In principle the source and center of unity, he is, as it were, so many men— separated by isolating layers more effective than steel or asbestos—divided into his differing diocesan commissions. We realize the exaggeration, but, at closer look, does it not have some correspondence to reality?

In Germany and Austria, the central (in name anyway) organization heading the different commissions is called the Pastoral Office. We do not pretend that this is all for the best, but permit us to say how, by itself, the name corresponds to the facts of an authentic pastoral theology. And it is permissible to think that all dioceses sorely need such an organization. The name has little bearing, provided that the unity of inspiration which it assures is the unity of the pastoral ministry. Only at this price will the paschal mystery regain its place.

4. INITIATION TO THE BIBLE AND SALVATION HISTORY

This apparently double initiation to the Bible and to salvation history is really a single reality, both necessarily taking place one within the other. Yet we must distinguish between them lest our understanding of one be sacrificed to our understanding of the other.

The biblical aspect of this reality has been summarized as follows:

1. The God of the Bible is not the God of the philosophers and the wise, but the God of Abraham, Isaac, and Jacob.

Biblical tradition does not take the form of a system, but of history, a succession of events connected one with another, progressively manifesting what St. Paul called "the mystery hidden in God and now revealed through the prophets."

God is conjointly the God Most High, inaccessible, whom no man has seen nor can see, and the God who intervenes in history.

2. In the Old Testament, God's interventions in history develop in three great stages. St. Matthew underscored their enumeration in his genealogy:

—First stage: Abraham and the patriarchs. The age of God's gratuitous promises demanding the response of faith.

—Second stage: Moses, David, the kingdom. Here there is a people, a territory, a law. This is the basis of an alliance by contract, a covenant.

—Third stage: exile and post-exilic period. In expiating their infidelities, the people become aware of their sinful condition. In their inability to satisfy justice, they long for Israel's redemption.

3. Appearing at the term of this history, in the fullness of time, Christ gathers in himself and realizes the religious content of these three ages: he saves the people from their sin (priest), he founds the true kingdom of God (king), he fulfills the promises (prophet). The whole economy of salvation is summed up in the paschal mystery in which Christ is king, priest, and prophet.

4. Since Easter, Christ's mystery expands in the Church. And then is God's wisdom, previously hidden, made manifest. And like Christ, the Church is defined by these three dimensions: the priestly, the royal, and the prophetic.

5. At the term of history, at the parousia, the mystery of the God of Abraham, Isaac, and Jacob will appear in its fullness: God will be definitively all in all.

6. The economy of salvation is not an aspect of revelation; it is revelation itself. Thus our faith is not based on a system of religious notions, but on God's interventions in history. The Creed refers directly to this economy: In the beginning God created the heavens and earth . . . under Pontius Pilate, the death and resurrection . . . today, the Holy Spirit animates the Church . . . at the end of time, the resurrection of the body.

It is essential and indispensable for every Christian to know the historical nature of revelation and redemption, as the Creed sums it up. In the last analysis, only in this perspective will it be possible fully to understand the paschal mystery as the summit and center of all. It seems useless to underline how fundamental this is to our question.

Yet this is not the only profit our faithful will gain. Initiation into the economy of salvation will also teach them the relationship between the Old Testament "types" and their realization in the fullness of time. This is a double advantage. On the one hand, the ancient "figures" will become so many "images" (or pictures) begetting in them an understanding of the different facets of the historical redemption deeper and more existential than all the more or less rational "explanations" that we can propound. On the other hand, a few brief instructions will be enough to understand the role and meaning of the numerous Lessons of Lent, Holy Week, and the paschal vigil. Inversely, experience has only too often shown both the difficulty in creating a "taste" for the depths of the paschal mystery, and the inconvenience caused the celebrant by these Lessons read and heard outside the great context of the economy of salvation.

This is for Easter and its immediate celebration. But there is the whole liturgical cycle already termed a kind of "sacrament" of salvation.

5. CELEBRATION

In the celebration of the sacrifice, there is an encounter, somehow a connection between two poles: the liturgical mystery and the Christian man. At the heart of this encounter there are elements, sprung from one or the other of these poles and providentially suited to one another, which interact. From this encounter and interaction the celebration draws its unique effectiveness extending to almost the entirety of a fully lived Christianity.

Dom Odo Casel has defined the liturgical mystery thus:

> The mystery is a sacred ritual action in which a saving deed is made present through the rite; the congregation, by performing the rite, takes part in the saving act, and thereby wins salvation.[9]

Our concern is twofold: first, that the liturgical mystery is an interaction on the part of celebrant and community, and second, that this interaction is accomplished by a rite always including, in some way, word and sign (material).

In the face of the liturgical mystery thus "realized" stands man, this being who, on earth, never exists except corporeally. We must, therefore, correctly understand this Incarnation. Body and soul are not two realities existing side by side. Their unity is

9. *The Mystery of Christian Worship*, p. 54.

an organic conjunction, not a mechanical proximity. Man is spirit incarnate and body animate. It would be a mistake, then, to see the body only as the soul's instrument. It is first of all the very way man exists, the form and expression of his existence in the world, the symbol of his spirit. There is, consequently, a constant interaction of one on the other, an influence of the body on the more spiritual faculties, and vice versa. Thus rises the profound and irreplaceable influence of symbol, of "image"; the importance of deeds, and attitudes, and, without doubt, also the meaning and value of the archetypes discovered by depth psychology. Pastoral theology has little noticed the profit which these could offer.[10]

Comparing these individual elements, either from the viewpoint of man or of liturgical mystery, one arrives at the following ideas:

Somehow the liturgical mystery is always itself essentially preaching (the word is never absent and a well-understood celebration gives it its rightful place), proclamation of the good news. Moreover, this is what St. Paul affirms in his famous text on the Eucharist: "As often as you shall eat this bread and drink this cup, you *proclaim* the death of the Lord, until he comes" (1 Cor. 11, 26). Obviously, the Apostle is not talking about an "announcement" made in words; it is made here in a bodily act of worship. The fact of eating the bread and drinking the cup, accompanied by the prayer, is itself a proclamation announcing the death of the Lord. While celebrating the Lord's Supper, the assembly bears witness to him and proclaims him present in his sacrifice and exaltation. Far from being merely a source of grace, the celebration is, at the same time, a proclamation. From this fact, Christianity is seen and known in its true nature: as an ever real history of salvation.

But there is more. The liturgical action appeals unceasingly to

10. See Josef Goldbrunner, *Individuation,* Notre Dame, 1964; and Louis Bouyer, *Rite and Man,* Notre Dame, 1962.

the "image," to the symbol, and it necessarily uses a whole ensemble of material things, such as water, bread, wine, and oil.

But far from being only the representation of a thing by our mental faculties, a representation perceived by human intelligence, the image is also an overflowing of the thing to which it refers, a revelation and manifestation of its essence, what might be called a "ray" that participates substantially in the thing itself. The image is the presentation of the very essence of that which is represented. The same is true of the symbol.

As for the elements which the liturgy borrows from material creation, they are themselves, and by themselves, but so many words. "All things were made through him, and without him was not anything made that was made" (Jn. 1, 3). All that exists, then, comes from the Word who is in God, and, therefore, everything has "the character of a word." The realities are not simple. They are no longer just simple significant facts placed in mute space. These are the words of the Creator-Speaker addressed to whoever "has ears to hear." The world proceeds not from power alone, not from thought alone, but from the word. The realities which it comprehends are so many words in which God the creator expresses their significance and translates them into the finite. These realities are always *in via,* searching for someone to understand them, someone who, through praising them, by giving thanks, and obeying, will find with Him who speaks the I-thou relation of creature with Creator.

Throughout the history of salvation, God has in some way taken care to state precisely a certain number of these thing-words, what he meant them to mean in the economy of revelation and salvation. Thus, for example, water "speaks" by itself of destruction, of life, of purification. But as the Church recalls in the prayer that consecrates the baptismal water, the word it naturally expresses becomes explicit:

Therefore, O water, created by the Almighty, I bless you by the living God, by the true God, by the holy God, by the God who through his word in the beginning separated you from the dry land and whose Spirit moved over you.

Who made you flow from a fountain in paradise and bade you water the whole earth with your four rivers; who in the desert changed your bitterness to sweetness so that you were fit to drink, and caused you to spring up out of a rock to quench the thirst of his people. I bless you also by our Lord Jesus Christ, his only-begotten Son, who by his power miraculously changed you into wine at Cana of Galilee; who walked upon your surface and was baptized in your Jordan stream by John; who caused you to flow, together with blood, out of his own side, and commanded his disciples to baptize believers in you, saying, "Go teach all nations, baptizing them in the name of the Father, and of the Son, and of the Holy Spirit."

To these we should add the other *magnalia Dei* recalled in the course of this same paschal night: the deluge, the passage through the Red Sea, that of the Jordan, etc.

In a way, there is a certain interpenetration of symbol and the "image," and it only reinforces their common power to signify.

In making use of exterior things, moreover, the celebration sets in motion, on man's part, not only his intellect, certainly, but his entire psychosomatic unity, and, in particular, the whole mysterious ensemble of archetypes. There is no need whatever to admit, with Jung, that these archetypes are the result of a collective experience of mankind in every age; in fact, it's difficult to see how such a "heritage" could exist. It just detracts from the fact the very existence of these fundamental dispositions of the human soul, present the world over, can no longer be called into doubt by anyone. We therefore find ourselves face to face with an admirable disposition of providence. The Creator who has made man and things, who "knows what is in man" and who understands the "word" he has entrusted to things, has prepared a profound accord, a miraculous correspondence, which he uses throughout the history of salvation and very particularly in the celebration of the liturgical mystery in order to communicate his Truth and his Life in an absolutely unique manner.

By the same fact, as Guardini notes,

. . . the bodily movements, the actions, and the material objects which it employs are all of the highest significance. It offers great opportunities of expression, of knowledge, and of spiritual experience; it is emancipating in its action, and capable of presenting a truth far more strongly and convincingly than can the mere word of mouth.[11]

Thus the liturgical celebration gives the Christian faithful the chance somehow to "experience" the truths of the faith which it proclaims and celebrates. Since it is action itself and makes the mystery celebrated affect the Christian, it is basically a privileged mode of knowledge by experience or participation. In it reality is reached by illumination and intuition. Far from being simply reflex, this sort of "vision" uses latent powers, arouses attention, and provokes fear and desire all at the same time. The "heart," in the sense in which St. Augustine and Pascal use the term, begins to understand.

How can we fail to recall in this context the experience of the disciples at Emmaus? St. Luke's Gospel is of special importance here. The risen Lord, whom the disciples had not recognized on the way even when he was interpreting to them "in all the Scriptures the things concerning himself," broke the bread and gave it to them, "and their eyes were opened and they recognized him" (Lk. 24, 27. 30–31). The evangelist seems to recall here the formula of Genesis 3, 7: "Then the eyes of both were opened." Thus, on two occasions, the celebration of a meal is the origin of knowledge, at first the knowledge of tragedy, and then this being replaced by blessed knowledge in the fullness of time. Towards the end of his account, St. Luke again remarks "how he was known to them in the breaking of the bread" (24, 35), an expression, at the time when the Gospel was written, which perhaps already had the technical significance which St. Luke seems to give it in the Acts (2, 42).

11. *The Church and the Catholic*, New York and London, 1940, p. 170.

The Church, in her turn, strikingly emphasizes this experience of the disciples, and that of all those who celebrate the Eucharist. In the alleluia hymn of the Second Sunday after Easter, she takes it up again, while adding slightly to the Gospel text: "The disciples recognized the Lord Jesus—in the breaking of the bread," and the alleluia follows up this thought with a verse from the day's Gospel: "I am the good shepherd: and I know my sheep, and mine know me" (Jn. 10, 14), which the Church repeats again in the communion hymn. The connections are clear: the Eucharistic meal celebrated "today" is the source of that unique knowledge called faith.

Rudolf Schnackenburg has written: "The primitive Church received from its liturgical life, and especially from the Eucharist, powerful impulses for its moral endeavor." [12] He thinks this is especially verified with regard to the disorders within the Church of Corinth that were rebuked by St. Paul (1 Cor. 11, 20–34). Their lack of consideration for the poor destroyed the fraternal communion and made it impossible to celebrate the "Lord's Supper," which essentially includes the fraternal reunion during the meal and Eucharist that follow. The attitude the Apostle is forced to condemn leads to an unworthy reception of the Eucharist, and makes one guilty of the Lord's body and blood. Paul asks each one, then, to examine himself seriously so that the Lord will no longer have to judge and condemn, for, to his mind, the numerous cases of sickness and death in the Church at Corinth are signs of a saving intervention of the Lord who wants to save the guilty community from the final judgment. We see how the Eucharist forms and educates each Christian particularly by the simultaneously realistic conception of the sacrament that it communicates (v. 29) and by the inseparable communitarianism of the whole body that it effects. The sacrament of unity is also the sacrament of fraternal love. No member of the faithful has the

12. *The Church in the New Testament,* New York and London, 1965, p. 44.

right to put himself above the ecclesial community; always starting from the obligation created by participation in the Lord's body and blood, and by the assembly forming only "one body" in the celebration of the Eucharist (10, 11), the Apostle enjoins those at Corinth who think or say that they are "strong": "Give no offense to Jews or Greeks or to the Church of God" (10, 32).

According to the Acts, the equally serious difficulties encountered at Jerusalem between "Hellenists" and "Hebrews" about daily help for the widows, had not succeeded in destroying the concord (Acts 6:16). As for Antioch, the incident mentioned in Galatians 2, 11–14, witnesses to his care lest the two groups, one Jewish in custom, the other Hellenistic, start taking the meal separately. In these two cases, the Eucharist is not expressly in question, but one senses that it underlies all the tensions: it imperiously demands unity.

In the Letter to the Ephesians, the prayer at the beginning of the letter (1, 3–14), the one immediately following (1, 15–19), the repeated allusions to the fact the community is the Lord's (1, 23; 2, 16; 3, 6; etc.), God's household (2, 19–22) in which all have access to the Father (2, 18; 3, 12) and in which all glory is, in common, by angels and men, given to God (3, 10. 20 ff.), in particular the whole passage on the unity in one body and one Spirit (4, 1–16)—show that St. Paul never ceased to think about a community assembled for divine worship. In fact, the Church of Ephesus received and read his letter in the liturgical assembly. Thus, needing to regulate the morality of his Christians, St. Paul very naturally selects from the liturgical life of the faithful essential themes on which to base his prescriptions.

The Ephesians have the experience of being members of one another (4, 25) when all eat the same bread and thus become one body. (see 1 Cor. 10, 17). Because of their baptism, received in the presence of the community, they know themselves marked with the seal of the Holy Spirit of God (4, 30). The phrase that speaks of Christ delivering himself for us in a sacrifice to God in fragrant odor (5, 2) seems to be a clear allusion to the sacrifice offered by the assembly. Add the invitation to thanksgiving, the appeal, "Awake, sleeper, and arise from among the dead, and Christ will enlighten" (5, 14), which probably applies to the day's baptismal liturgy—this is why the Church, filled with the Holy Spirit in the liturgical celebration, appears at the end of the chapter as the accomplishment of all that God has done for man. Just as the essence of God is the community of the three Persons, the unending joy, the Son returns to the Father in the Spirit, so the new situation of redeemed man is nothing other than the fraternal community filled with the same joy which God possesses. The Christians mingle their voices in the eternal thanksgiving. The Son returns to the Father when, filled with the Spirit of the Lord Jesus Christ, they return thanks to the Father. They share in this thanksgiving only because they are united in one body in the Lord, and only in this way can they present themselves before the Father in the name of Christ.

Starting directly from this experience of the celebration, the apostle goes on to regulate all the duties, great and small, presenting themselves in the daily life of the Christians. From the unity that rules the body of Christ, the great community of the Church, he passes on to the unity which should exist in the small family community (Ch. 5).

For those who "have eyes to see," it is not difficult to show how the apostolic experience, such as the letters transmit it to us, can be ours. For one thing, the genuine celebration is the place where many Christians discover and understand their call to "commitment." This discovery can, of course, have other origins. But we think that, in general, the calls to militant Catholicism that arise from the celebration are more authentic and enduring.

We see the opposite phenomenon as well. In the celebration, unfortunately, the inevitable "discernment of spirits" occurs (see Chapter 10 of St. Matthew): sensing, as they themselves admit, where the authentic celebration would lead with all its necessary exigencies, some prefer something easier, and it is honesty on their part not to come again at all. One will understand, we feel sure, to what degree this chapter on the celebration was necessary in the context of this work. If our faithful have to regain a living faith in the paschal mystery attracting their "heart" as much as their intelligence, if their moral life, their Christian life must very shortly become "paschal" again in the sense that we have described, then the celebration must play an irreplaceable role.

Still, this celebration must be true, that is, it must strictly obey its own proper laws. Unfortunately, this cannot be said to be the general practice. There is no question of recalling here one by one the various elements of celebration and expressing the laws of each. Nevertheless, we think it will be at least useful, if not necessary, to show with the help of several examples how people risk committing extremely serious mistakes in this area. For instance, what is usually the obvious thing at a "directed Mass"? The celebrant becomes a "bit player" who is "doing his part" at the altar, while the "director" monopolizes the attention of the assembly and "does" certain things more or less in agreement with the actions taking place on the altar. We could not imagine a more effective method of killing active participation. The institution of "commentator" is certainly excellent in itself, but regrettably the too often use of one individual as commentator— despite good intentions, which in any case is beside the point— increases tenfold the ill effects of the ancient "directors" who became "commentators" and believed that they were allowed to do nearly anything. Thus the question: Most of the time, would it not be better if the celebrant himself took charge of the "coaching"?

In sum, the problem of celebration is not as simple as it might at first appear. "Practical" as celebration is, it is not a matter of "practice" or "experience." An authentic celebration is possible only if it is based on sound theology. A key element in celebration is preaching—more precisely, the homily.

6. THE HOMILY

How is preaching to be reformed? Christ himself showed us how when he preached in the synagogue at Nazareth. St. Luke has preserved the scene for us. Participating one Sabbath in the weekly assembly, Jesus rose to read. In the book of the prophet Isaiah which they gave him, he came across the text describing his own messianic character and work (Is. 61, 1–2). After he finished the proclamation, he sat down and declared: "Today this scripture has been fulfilled in your hearing" (Lk. 4, 21).

It seems to us correct to see in this episode the "type" of every sacramental celebration and, most especially, that of the Eucharist. In the two cases, even if the appearances differ, the reality remains the same. In the sacramental celebration, there is, as in the synagogue at Nazareth, both the word, and the presence of the redeeming Christ. It is obvious in regard to the word. As for the presence of the Lord, we know that the appearances of the risen Lord were, of course, meant to manifest the resurrection, but every bit as much also to teach the disciples that, from now on, the Master who deprived them of his physical presence would be "in their midst" by means of a new kind of presence. This in the very exercise of his messianic powers which is now entrusted to the Church. Thus, St. Leo could affirm: "What was visible of our redeemer has passed over into the sacraments." [13]

At Nazareth as in the sacramental celebration, the word and the sacramental sign have some connection, almost identical roles. The Jews assembled in the synagogue saw a man very much like themselves and whom they knew well: "Is this not the son of Joseph?", they said. This man is also the one whom the prophet proclaimed; this human body so familiar to his fellow citizens is the sacramental "sign," the "primordial" sacrament, the

13. "Second Sermon on the Ascension of the Lord."

source of all the others, simultaneously revealing and veiling the Son of God present and acting in it. Yet they must be told this so that those who see it will be able to understand and believe. And they must be told in two ways, one as essential as the other: by the proclamation of the word of God on the one hand, clarifying somewhat the nature and mission of this "sign;" and, on the other, by what is already the homily, which is absolutely indispensable for making the connection between the word proclaimed and the "sign" presented: "Today this Scripture has been fulfilled in your hearing."

The same is true for the whole sacramental celebration. It presents a sign to the faithful. At baptism there is water, having, in its own right, a certain significance. We indicated earlier how every created thing is a "word," and how, moreover, throughout the history of salvation, God has taken care to state this "word" precisely. For this reason, above all, it seems to us that "it is part of the very essence of a sign to need explanation." [14] In the case of the baptismal water, naturally signifying death, the origin of life, purification, etc., the mystagogical word ought to state precisely which death, which life, and which purification it is dealing with. And for it to become "the regenerating water" of baptism, the words of the profession of faith and, actually, those of the baptismal formulary, must join in declaring that "Today all these passages of the Scripture are fulfilled," evoked by the sign of the water. For even if in the case of baptism the "word" is not, strictly speaking, the word of God extracted textually from the Scriptures, it is "pronounced as the conclusion to the whole disclosure of God's word which reaches its climax in the Gospel," and in it "is accomplished the coming of that same word in Christ to Israel in the fullness of time." [15]

Inversely, one could say—fundamentally the same thing—

14. Max Brändle, "Kommentar (Auferstehung Jesu)," in *Orientierung, Katholische Blätter*, April, 1962.

15. Louis Bouyer, *Liturgical Piety*, p. 110.

that God's Word which, "just as from the heavens the rain and snow come down and do not return there till they have watered the earth making it fertile and fruitful, giving seed to him who sows and bread to him who eats," will not return to God void, without having done his will and fulfilled its mission (Is. 55, 10–11); God's Word takes flesh and, somehow, is "summed up" in the sacramental sign. From all the evidence, such was the case at the synagogue at Nazareth. In a special way, the same is true for the Eucharist, where the proclamation of the story of the institution becomes, if one can say this, the narration of what is really happening at the very moment this Word is announced.

In regard to the Eucharist, our great interest is that it involves a double sacramental word. In the strict sense, it is evidently the account of the institution. But in the Eucharistic celebration taken as a whole, the whole liturgy of the word is also sacramental, even though, in another way, it is only the account of the institution.

Unfortunately, despite the undeniable progress made in this area in the last twenty or thirty years, we cannot say that this essential relation between the two "parts" of the Mass has in general been completely understood. As long as this direct continuity is not entirely perceived and as long as people fail to draw all the consequences out, our celebrations will not be what they ought to be. Not only is the "testament" of the Lord not carried out, but, moreover, the Christian people remain subject to a regime of undernourishment. If one is looking for causes for actual dechristianization, here is one of them, one of the most decisive yet it is hardly ever mentioned. For several centuries, despite the efforts of the Council of Trent to make a lie of it,[16] the terrible assertion of the prophet remains true: "The babes cry for good: but there is no one to give it to them" (Lam. 4, 4).

It is of the greatest importance, then, fully to rediscover this

16. Session XXII; Denzinger, no. 946.

fundamental tie uniting the liturgy of the word and the liturgy of the Eucharist. At the same time, we must see it in the light of the relation existing, *mutatis mutandis,* between the sacramental word and the sacramental sign. Every comparison is inexact to some degree, but, with this reservation, what was said above about the episode at Nazareth and about baptism is just as true in regard to the Eucharist.

The celebration of the word has the irreplaceable mission of "specifying" the sacramental celebration's meaning, substance, and effects. It is well understood that the word itself brings a certain presence: "The Apostle is present, the Lord is present. The lesson causes such and such a saving event to take place, in truth, today." [17] And yet, in the sacramental order in which the Eucharist is set, this word ought to "realize" itself in the sacrament, where it finds its full presence and effectiveness. "The word of God is the proclamation in the Church of the mystery of salvation which the Eucharist realizes." [18]

The Christian must know well that "as often as you eat this bread and drink the cup, you proclaim the Lord's death until he comes" (1 Cor. 11, 26), and since each Eucharist includes, with the presence of the Lord, the presence of his whole redemptive work, it is practically impossible for him to "realize" this infinite fullness. So the Church undertook very early to develop it, on the one hand by multiplying feasts of the Lord, besides Sunday and the feast of Easter, and on the other by choosing for each Sunday and feast lessons aimed at concretizing such and such an aspect of the total mystery which she intends to celebrate and communicate in a special way. With all her authority, then, she says what "is going on" in this Mass.

The very essence of the Eucharist demands, therefore, the proclamation of the word of God in an effective and intelligible

17. A. G. Martimort, *L'Eglise en prière,* Paris, 1946, p. 114.
18. *Directoire pour la pastorale de la messe* (of the French hierarchy), no. 1.

127

manner, in every Mass—even when there are only a few people there. The faithful's individual reading with the help of their missals cannot take its place. God's word is addressed essentially to the Church community, and, in every way, faith is born "from what is heard" (Rom. 10, 17). To read, even in a loud enough voice, the texts of the missal, constitutes neither a proclamation nor, all the more, an intelligible proclamation. This brings in a technique, an attitude, a tone, and poses the problem of the vernacular. The solution—near, we hope—depends on the Church. However, she gives us at least enough latitude to preserve the essence.[19]

Even if done to perfection, this proclamation cannot suffice. The Lord was not content with it in the synagogue at Nazareth, and rightly. God's word, once proclaimed, calls for the homily as its indispensable complement. The homily is in some way the hinge by which word and sacrament are joined. To it has fallen the task of declaring, "Today this Scripture has been fulfilled in your hearing," and of explaining how.

There is more. What is "fulfilled today" in the Eucharistic celebration never appears clearly in the texts proclaimed. The literal sense of the gospels describes such and such an historical fact which, as such, will never repeat itself. The Lord no longer is born "today" in Bethlehem; no longer is he "today" calming the tempest disturbing the sea; no longer is he "today" raising to life the young man of Naim. So also, his death, his birth, and his miracles were done once and for all (see Rom. 6, 10). Moreover, the Gospels of Christmas eve, of the Fourth Sunday after the Epiphany, and of the Fifteenth Sunday after Pentecost, chosen by the Church to be the "sacramental word" of the Eucharist celebrated on these days, cannot have as their purpose—as so many

19. See the instruction *Sacred Music and the Sacred Liturgy* of the Sacred Congregation of Rites, in Seasoltz, *The New Liturgy*, pp. 255–282, esp. pp. 280–281 (Article 112).

sermons seem to say—to stir up feelings about the little infant in the crib, to show us the power of the Lord, or to make us see his kindness to the widow of Naim.

The word of God, completely filled with the fullness of the eternal word, somehow is composed of several levels, penetrating and clarifying one another. Under the surface of the literal sense—in which this viewpoint keeps all its validity and importance—she encloses a "spiritual" sense which, even if it were not perceived by the sacred author himself, has nonetheless been willed by God.[20] In choosing Scripture texts, in relating them, in the formulary, to other texts from the Scriptures, and in proclaiming them thus as the sacramental word of the Eucharist, the Church, the authorized interpreter of the Scriptures, lays open a sense which, though without doubt very close to the "spiritual" sense, seems nevertheless somewhat different: we willingly call it the "mysterious" sense of the Scriptures.

We must go still further. In these texts, God speaks "today," that is, at a precise moment in salvation history. This word, dealing only with the Eucharist, constitutes an "acceptable time," a unique intervention of God like the *magnalia Dei* of the old covenant which the sacraments have, in their turn, replaced. In a certain sense, then, God has never pronounced this word again in the same way and never will, and thus he charged it with a unique meaning, valid for this very moment of salvation history, because it reveals and realizes a unique aspect of the Eucharist's total perfection.

The homily's role is to draw out and announce this "mysterious" sense set down in the patristic tradition and suggested by the Church herself through the context. For she places the Gospel pericope in a context shaped around the Eucharist itself, the memory and presence of the whole redeeming mystery. It is

20. See the encyclical *Divino afflante Spiritu* of Pius XII, Article 27.

suggested, too, by the whole formulary and by the liturgical "season." In bringing out this sense—and in this alone—can the homily affirm: "Today this passage of the Scriptures has been fulfilled."

When the faithful come to understand, with the help of the homily, the *hodie* of the mystery; when, thus, they feel truly concerned and in some way "embarked" on the splendors of the celebrated mystery, then do they "set foot on the foundation." In fact, in the parishes where the homily is well-handled, there is an atmosphere of prayer so profound that it surprises those unaccustomed to it. As they confirm—the faithful are very sensitive to this—this atmosphere is lost as soon as, for example, a strange preacher "did not show how this happens," as a young peasant told us on the feast day of a patron saint (he meant to say: how the word is accomplished in the eucharistic liturgy).

The problem of the celebration as such has been brought in only because it is called to play an essential role in the paschal renewal of the parish and of the whole Christian life. We must learn to realize that, among the many, varied means that have been brought up, the homily occupies a primary and irreplaceable position. Even before the ever-needed mystagogy—always on some aspect or other of the paschal mystery specified by the lessons—it must ceaselessly return to this central mystery of Christianity. At the same time, since it has to show that "Today this passage of Scripture has been fulfilled," it must succeed, slowly and step by step, in making the Christian people conscious of the *hodie* of the liturgical mystery.

IV

THE PASCHAL MYSTERY
AND THE PEOPLE OF GOD

Our intention in this chapter will be to demonstrate by means of a few concrete and important examples how an enlightened and inspired pastoral ministry can give a parish a true paschal character and make the people of Christ understand what it means to live a paschal faith.

1. THE LITURGICAL CYCLE

On the parish level one primary, urgent task is to make the reality of the liturgical cycle comprehensible and alive. Today Christian people seem to have lost their sense of mystery, and a great deal of work needs to be done to restore this sense. Education is one means, but more important is the celebration of the word, specifically the homily.

Then we must correct certain viewpoints distorted by accretions such as the double feast of Christmas and Epiphany— accretions which, although they are enriching in themselves, nevertheless obscure how the entire cycle centers on the paschal mystery.

To succeed in inculcating in the faithful a more correct view of the liturgical year, we must first of all remove from missals, catechisms, and sermons the erroneous ideas and terms of a Pentecostal or a Christmas or an Easter cycle. We must speak of one cycle only: the celebration of the economy of salvation whose summit is the feast of Easter. There will be difficulties, at least for a while: practical divisions will be lost. In particular, whatever the cost, the First Sunday of Advent will have to be torn from the place it so tenaciously holds in the minds of the faithful.

Welcome or not, this again brings up the inevitable problem: When, therefore, does the liturgical year actually begin? There is more here than simply the pleasant fancies of liturgists. If there be a fear of innovation for innovation's sake, this question yet remains undeniably central to the great problem which occupies us.

We would not be so imprudent as to resort to historical arguments—for there are none. But then history cannot be used in support of the present division either. We have already very briefly recounted the amorphous, even somewhat haphazard way the present liturgical year gradually evolved. If, during certain ages, in liturgical books a beginning date was set—they had to begin somewhere—whether in January or on the first Sunday of Advent, or even on Septuagesima depended more on historical accidents (for example, the beginning of the civil year) than on considerations having anything to do with the theological or mystical order. But one fact is certain: that Easter, despite its variable date, is the center of the year; and the greater part of the cycle is constructed about, is centered on this movable feast.

If, then, the liturgical year allows the Christian to relive each year the economy of salvation, how can the Christian do so if the liturgical year is not some sort of "sacrament," the re-presentation of this economy of salvation from its beginning (the creation, re-presented at Septuagesima) to its end (the parousia, sacramentally anticipated at Christmas and Epiphany)?

132

In this way, and in this way only, can he go "up to Jerusalem" (Lk. 18, 31), with all past generations, the catechumens of past and present, to relive during Lent his own initiation into the paschal mystery by baptism,—to live Easter, the summit of salvation economy, to participate in the redemption's extension to the whole world and all mankind. The kingdom inaugurated in the passover of the Lord during the "time of the Church" mysteriously lives between the Ascension and the Seventeenth Sunday after Pentecost (and from the Eighteenth Sunday to the Sunday of the Epiphany). Throughout all this time, the Christian integrates himself into that essential expectation of the return of the glorious Lord, a "stranger and traveller" in those "last times," though already partially in possession of the things to come.

The suppression of a so-called "cycle of Christmas" and, concurrently, the conscious celebration of the parousia at Christmas and Epiphany seems required just as much by a fact of primary importance in the theological and liturgical orders. It is certain, in fact, that the paschal mystery and the mystery of the parousia are the same mystery, but under different aspects. In other words, the parousia is not just one of the multiple aspects of the one paschal mystery, on the same level as the death, resurrection, and ascension of the Lord and the mission of the Spirit. It is true that the Lord separated these different aspects of his life by periods of time of varying length, and the Church, in turn, separated them in her annual celebration. Would she, then, fail to celebrate everything but the parousia? This would be a very serious omission on the part of the Church, for it could not be that the only part of the whole mystery uncelebrated is the part which gives reason for its existence.

From a pastoral point of view, all the consequences would be, and in fact are, equally grave. If the Christian people have lost even the memory of the essential eschatological dimension of Christianity, if the general resurrection is considered to be nothing more than a theoretical dogma hardly concerning them at all, if they are no longer at all aware as was St. Paul that the redemption consists in the fact that Jesus will save us at the time of the final judgment, then we must look for the cause above all in the present idea of Christmas cycle and Christmas feast as a unique remembrance of the Lord's first coming. As a consequence of this idea the paschal mystery under the aspect of the parousia no longer plays a part in the celebration.

Furthermore, this is actually the whole theme of the cycle; the formularies of the Sundays and feasts exemplify this. Between the Twenty-Fourth Sunday after Pentecost and the First Sunday of Advent, there is no real break at all (as there would inevitably be if there were at that point an end and a new beginning); rather, there is an admirable continuity marked by the double Gospel on the "end of the world" (Mt. 24, 15–35, and Lk. 21, 25–33). The hope filling the Masses of the Advent Sundays is our own, "today." The acclamations of the Masses of Christmas and Epiphany, in their true and full sense, are addressed to the King of Glory. The epistles of the Sundays after the Epiphany unceasingly demand charity, because the "Wedding Feast of the Lamb" has come and the one thing the Bridegroom demands of the bride is that she love him.

All these clearly point out to what extent the liturgical cycle, thus understood and lived, makes the unique place and complete dominance of the paschal mystery obvious: Easter is truly the center of all the preparations of the Old Testament and this year. From it radiates each aspect of the redemption to develop itself during the "age of the Church" (and its re-presentation, this year) and to lead to its total fulfillment at the parousia. This will not be something entirely new. What will be new is the open manifestation to all humankind of what already has been potentially acquired: the Lordship of Jesus and the participation of the redeemed in his glory, the fruit of Easter, acquired once and for all when the Father "highly exalted him and bestowed on him the name which is above every name, that at the name of Jesus every knee should bow, in heaven and on earth and under the earth, and every tongue confess that Jesus Christ is Lord" (Phil. 2, 9–11).

It would therefore be at least very useful, not to say indispensable, to celebrate Advent, Christmas, and the Epiphany in this perspective: the coming in the flesh as commemorative, a figure of the coming in glory. If we reach this point, Easter will regain its true place, since we are already trying to break down the unfortunate competition between the feasts of Christmas and Easter existing in the minds of the faithful.

Moreover, it will be then possible to solve another pastoral problem of great importance. It is a fact that the majority of the faithful think each liturgical cycle relates only to itself; that from one year to the next, therefore, there is no change at all, that each feast of Easter, of Christmas, and so forth, remains indefinitely the same feast of Easter or Christmas. The conception we advocate lets the faithful see more easily that the economy of salvation is actually "one-way," the liturgical cycle being a sort of ascending spiral, a pathway winding ever upward around the holy mountain of God, to reach the summit in the glory of the parousia—or, to use another image: a sort of downward spiral taking us deeper and deeper into the mystery of the redemption.

2. THE SACRAMENTS

Since the sacraments are essentially paschal it is of necessity this be brought home, as much in catechizing and preaching as in the celebration of the sacraments themselves.

(A) The Eucharist

History is irreversible. We no longer see a single Eucharistic feast, reserved for Sunday and celebrated by the bishop for the whole community. Without wishing to be in any way critical of the later development and actual state of affairs to which this has led, we can regret in particular the disappearance of this tacit yet eloquent affirmation of the unity between Sunday and the Eucharist. It served by its very nature to make the eminently paschal character of both Sunday and the Eucharist obvious. In the present situation, we must find other means of attaining the same end.

The Eucharist has many aspects. The reaction to the Reformation emphasized (very much to the point) its sacrificial aspect, but unfortunately at the expense of its character as a meal. Then, too, we wonder how many of our faithful realize that it is, as its name indicates, "Thanksgiving," and live as such. It seems reasonable that if more accent were placed on its paschal nature of the Eucharist, the faithful would come to a more balanced view of these different aspects, and simultaneously understand them better. Above all, here too the paschal mystery would regain its place. Catechetics, but specifically preaching, not special sermons on the Mass but daily homilies, might be one means of restoring the paschal nature of the Eucharist in the minds of the faithful.

(B) Baptism

The celebration of baptism offers magnificent possibilities only if accompanied by a mystagogy (a commentary on the mystery aspect involved) that underlines the presentation of the paschal mystery made present by the sacrament. In most parishes, moreover, it is possible to administer baptism, from time to time during the year, before Sunday high Mass, with the parish already congregated. But the mystagogy is indispensable—there should be either no homily or a very short one since the baptism takes its place magnificently, and the celebration should end with the Asperges announced as the weekly renewal of baptism. The points thus stressed are these: the deep ties which baptism has with Sunday and therefore with Easter; that it is an initiation into the community of God's people; that it is the introduction to the Eucharist, giving the participation in the priesthood of the people which enables the Christian to offer the Eucharist with the ordained priest.

(C) Marriage, Anointing of the Sick, Penance

To atempt such a review of all the sacraments would take too long. Let us just say that it is always possible—and always necessary—to indicate in one way or another their profound relation to the paschal mystery. It is enough to use the possibilities continually presenting themselves, even if this consists in nothing more than pointing out that the holy oils, used in their administration, are blessed in the course of the chrism Mass on Holy Thursday.

But let us delay over two of these sacraments for which, at first sight at least, this might seem more difficult. During the rite of marriage, the priest can, in the address and in the homily—these two are, in fact, necessary—take his lead from the epistle, proclaiming this sacrament's mystery "great in Christ and in the Church." He can show how it is eminently paschal, a figure of the Church, the bride of Christ, born on the cross from the Lord's opened side. In the second instance, at the time of the anointing of the sick, circumstances occasionally allow some explanation of the mystery. This would be the moment to show how the sacrament exhibits the profound relationship with the baptism (and penance) it completes.

Regarding the sacrament of penance, it would be worth-while to emphasize in catechesis its character as "laborious baptism," the phrase Trent took from the Fathers.[1] It might also be well to recall a forgotten rubric of the pontifical that the bishop exhort his priests in synod to invite the faithful to come to confession for Ash Wednesday. There would here be two possibilities for pointing out the paschal ties of this sacrament, and it would perhaps also hold the solution for the problem of Easter confessions. In addition, the sacrament of penance gives us a marvelous occasion to nourish a paschal spirituality in the faithful.

3. THE CELEBRATION OF LENT, EASTER, AND "BLESSED PENTECOST"

From all evidence, the work involved in returning the paschal mystery to its rightful place in the ministry should bear primarily on the celebration of Lent, Easter, and "Blessed Pentecost."

(A) Lent

There is no true paschal (and especially vigil) celebration without the preparation of Lent. This is an obvious fact, and the Church's uninterrupted tradition confirms it—if there be any such need.

Conversely, Lent can be understood only as springing from Easter and dependent on it; for the faithful, its participants, it is a

1. Session XIV, Chapter 2; Denzinger, no. 895.

paschal celebration, a true "passage" with the Lord, consciously lived as such and through the liturgy. First of all, therefore, Lent should be understood and lived as a "liturgical," sacramental liturgy. It is the time of the "venerable solemnities of fasting," and it befits us to enter into these solemnities piously and in secure devotion.[2]

More than an undertaking of man, Lent is the work of God.[3] In other words, far from being a mere preparation for Easter, Lent already is, in some way, the beginning of the celebration of that feast (a celebration which is completed only at Pentecost). On Ash Wednesday, God speaks in the lesson: "Then the Lord became jealous for his land, and had pity on his people. The Lord answered and said to his people, 'Behold, I am sending to you grain, wine, and oil, and you will be satisfied' " (Joel 2, 18–19). The essential element of Lent is the "sacramental world" symbolized here by these prophetic "images," especially the wheat, the food of the Eucharist, the oil of the Spirit. The sacrament of penance and the "sacrament of the word" are in Lent dispensed more abundantly than during the rest of the year. Conversion, penance, fasting should begin here and here return. These sacraments themselves, on this basis become truly and profoundly liturgy. Springing from the Eucharist above all and returning to it, they are, even in Lent, "death with Christ" and the beginning of the paschal dynamism leading to participation in the resurrection.

This is the perspective from which our ministry should make Lent live for our faithful. Whatever form their mortification

2. Entrance Prayer of the Mass of Ash Wednesday. The *Maryknoll Missal* translates it thus: "O Lord, may the faithful begin the solemn season of fast with fitting piety, and may they continue through to its end with unwavering devotion."

3. A fact underlined in some way in almost all the Masses of the ferial days of Lent. See, for example, the Entrance Prayer of Tuesday of the Second Week: "O Lord, fulfill in us the benefits of the holy Lenten fast. Teach us our duties and assist us with your grace to perform them."

assumes, it should be integral with liturgy, not some kind of competitive sport. We should introduce children not so much to the idea of "making sacrifices" (which, moreover, forever distorts their idea of sacrifice), but to the more correct understanding that fasting consists first of all in "denying themselves their own will." [4] In their case, this consists primarily in obeying their parents more readily and so forth.

We priests, too, should know we have no right to abuse these *veneranda solemnia,* to arrange them to our individual liking (certain retreats and "special devotions," even if Lent itself is, as essentially communal, the great and irreplaceable paschal retreat), and to substitute what we think we cannot "get across" at any other time. This is especially important in preaching. The "Lenten sermon" is not to be used to treat a "topic" important as it may seem to us. The true Lenten sermon, the only one possible, is the Sunday homily; also, since it is now possible, the homily during the week at the evening Mass. Both should draw on the texts of these Masses.

(B) *Holy Week, the Vigil, and Easter*

We have already shown how much the formation of a double triduum—joined with other causes—distorted the understanding of the paschal mystery. When Good Friday and Holy Saturday are completely cut off from Easter (and from the vigil) in their respective celebrations, we fail to see the fundamental unity really existing between the Lord's death and resurrection, as well as the dynamism flowing one from the other. Unfortunately, the new code of rubrics has maintained this regrettable dichotomy.

It is all the more important, therefore, repeatedly to emphasize, during the preparation and the celebration itself, the deep

4. Is. 58, 13 (Vulgate). Reading of the Saturday after Ash Wednesday.

unity of the paschal mystery, delineated somehow in successive periods, as much on the historical plane as on the level of the liturgical "memorial."

This is no easy task and it will take time: it goes against the grain of ideas deeply imbedded in minds and hearts. Yet it is not impossible. The liturgy itself never ceases to offer occasions when, for example, a well-put comment could underline the unity of the mystery. Thus, on Good Friday, the introduction of the singing of the passion would reassert the sovereign liberty of the Lord who himself dominated and directed the events, and did not simply undergo them. The comment preceding the veneration of the cross would describe its triumphant aspect. Similarly, it would be possible to highlight the numerous details already announcing the victory of the resurrection, not forgetting the ancient "your cross" which mentions it expressly. These several indications for Good Friday are given as examples. Every day of Holy Week, especially the paschal vigil, offers like opportunities. If the pastor is himself permeated by the unity of the paschal mystery, if he lives it in his celebration, it will be easy for him to discover and use this inherent unity.

The priest should give his wholehearted attention and care to the celebration of the vigil. All the preparations during Lent—in some way the parish liturgy throughout the liturgical year—should emphasize the essential place of Easter during the liturgical year.

(C) The "Holy Fifty Days"

It is undoubtedly better to use the ancient terminology as much to avoid confusion as to incite interest in something the Church of the first centuries simply assumed, something today which is totally forgotten: the "mysterious" reality of the "fifty days" after

Easter, an integral part of the paschal mystery and its celebration.

During these fifty days the mystery and the joy of Easter continue. Moreover, this is attested by the witness of the liturgy itself, especially by the very fact of the Easter octave. The magnificent Masses are testimony to the resurrection (epistles), chant the victory of baptism and new life (the chants), and glow with the renewed apparitions of the Risen Lord (Gospels). But this is no less true of Pentecost. We have already said: one did not fast or genuflect.[5] He continued to wear the white garments. Other more essential facts translate the profound reality in which these more exterior details are rooted. In the Gospels, all taken from St. John, the Sunday liturgy ceaselessly proclaims the "I go to the Father" of the Lord, really the very essence of the paschal mystery.[6] The Second Sunday after Pentecost picks up the mystery of the redemption in the image of the Good Shepherd who has given up his life for his sheep and thus given them life. Since the fourth century, in the ancient Pentecost, two feasts are especially important: the Ascension and Pentecost. These commemorate less the corresponding historical facts than they illuminate two essential aspects of the paschal mystery—the Lord's exaltation and the sending of the Spirit, given in the passage "out of this world to the Father" (Jn. 13, 1). This explains very happily the preface of the Ascension: the Lord has been exalted in the heavens to make us "partakers of his divinity." As to Pentecost, it was solemnized very early, not as a feast of the Holy Spirit, but inasmuch as it is the last day of the "fifty" to celebrate the communication of the Spirit, precisely the "fruit" of Easter.[7]

5. So, also, during this time, the suppression of the *flectamus genua,* the custom of saying the antiphon "Regina Caeli" standing, and for the same reason, the prescription to say the "Angelus" on Sunday, weekly during Easter, standing.

6. Third Sunday: Jn. 16, 16–22; Fourth Sunday: Jn. 16, 5–14; Fifth Sunday: Jn. 16, 23–30.

7. See Jungmann, *Public Worship,* pp. 202 ff.

Thus the liturgy witnesses clearly that Pentecost continues the celebration of the paschal mystery. And this witness is weighty, not only because, in the words of Pius XI, the liturgy is "the most important organ of the ordinary magisterium of the Church," but also and especially because its sacramental realism re-presents what it proclaims.

We thought we should insist at some length on this problem of the "holy fifty days." We greatly need a true "restoration"; without it, Holy Week will really remain unfulfilled. This restoration is necessary, first of all, to assure a complete celebration of the paschal mystery as the liturgy conceives of it, but also, and just as important, that the paschal mystery may be understood and lived fully. Most likely, no one would dare contest the fact that the faithful know only a few of the glorifying effects, essential as they are, of the paschal mystery—even the effects on Jesus himself. Pentecost with its unceasing refrain of "I go to the Father," its first apex on the feast of the Ascension, is to teach them precisely this: exaltation is integral to the resurrection. "God has made him . . . Lord" St. Peter testifies (Acts 2, 36); because he "emptied himself, . . . and became obedient unto death, . . . God has highly exalted him and bestowed on him the name [Kyrios] which is above every name, that at the name of Jesus every knee should bow . . ." (Phil. 2, 7 ff.).

How many Christians really know that the paschal mystery is not complete without the giving of the Spirit, the gift of the "last days," that the redemption consists in the very giving of the Spirit, for the Spirit is "himself the remission of all sins," [8] the principle of the new life?

Yet, these dimensions are just as essential to the paschal mystery as its eschatological dimension are. The demand is imperative to rediscover these facets in our vigil celebration and its

---

8. Post-Communion of Tuesday after Pentecost Sunday.

final, though only sacramental, fulfillment in Advent and the feasts of Christmas and Epiphany. Again, our faithful need not only prolong the paschal joy in order simply to live it more fully than the short moments of the vigil itself, but they must come to know the Pentecostal celebration as an "image" of heavenly life, "paradise regained," the "new creation," not just promises but a reality now actually begun. In other words, if the forty days of Lent represent the life of this world, the fifty days of Pentecost represent the life of the "world to come" already begun.

Thus, in a well-understood paschal celebration, centered on Holy Week and especially the vigil, Pentecost would be in a way dependent on Quadragesima. And would not the best way to bring about this rediscovery of the meaning of Pentecost perhaps be to explain that Lent, rather than a preparation, is already a beginning of the celebration?

No one doubts that this "restoration" of the "blessed Pentecost" will long remain among the most difficult task of the parish liturgy. In fact, this will be more than a re-creation, since it literally must start from nothing. It nevertheless seems possible. The numerous, obvious restorative elements we have already enumerated: well-written homilies; the emphasis on the importance of the Sundays after Easter, above all Ascension and Pentecost (an importance clearly surpassing that of Corpus Christi and the feast of the Sacred Heart); the presentation of these two feasts in their paschal context; and so forth. These will not fail, in the long run, to return to Pentecost its due place and importance.